PROVEN WAYS
TO A
SUCCESSFUL
CHURCH

Al Stauderman
and
Jim Morentz

ABINGDON
Nashville

FORTY PROVEN WAYS TO A SUCCESSFUL CHURCH

Library of Congress Cataloging in Publication Data

Stauderman, Albert P.
  Forty proven ways to a successful church.

  1.   Church management.   2.   Church publicity.
3. Pastoral theology. I.   Morentz, James W., joint
author.   II.   Title.
BV652.S68   254   80-12604

ISBN 0-687-13295-9 (pbk.)

MANUFACTURED BY THE PARTHENON PRESS
NASHVILLE, TENNESSEE, UNITED STATES OF AMERICA

To Dodd and Doris

for years of patience and understanding
Al and Jim

Contents

SECTION IV   INCREASING INCOME

Don't Sit Down

This book is meant to be read on the run. It is an action book to solve problems and make things happen in your church. Feel free to borrow and adapt anything you find in these pages. Provide copies of the book to your stewardship committees, your educational leaders, your council members, your musicians. Tear out the sample material and take it to your printer. Make this book work for you!

We believe that sound Christian teaching underlies every project suggested here. However, we have deliberately omitted doctrinal or theological discussion, because this is a book of practical, common-sense advice. Each project described here works. It has been tried successfully in a congregation. It will work for you if you wholeheartedly follow the directions. That's a guarantee!

Many of the projects contained here were developed in three Lutheran churches—St. Paul, Teaneck, New Jersey; First Church, Pittsburgh, Pennsyl-vania, and First Church, Los Angeles, California. Special appreciation is owed to those congregations. Sample materials also come from St. Mark Church, Dunedin, Florida, and Providence Church, Lexington, South Carolina. We realize that some of these projects may already have been put into practice in churches elsewhere.

When you've used ideas from this book with success in your parish and feel a glow of accomplishment, the authors would like to know about it. Please write and tell us. And if you have other good ideas that have been effective in your parish, we'd like to hear about those, too. Address Al and Jim, Box 360B, Cresco, Pennsylvania 18326.

The Christian faith works best when it is lived out in the daily affairs of Christ's people. The ideas in this book will be effective only when you put them to work in the life of your parish. So get busy!

Al and Jim

Section I

Increasing Attendance

1.

Liven Up Your Festivals!

Some Sundays in the year create a little ripple in congregations when they ought to be creating a tidal wave. Times like Mother's Day, Thanksgiving, Pentecost, or days of baptisms or confirmations are all "special" to some degree, but why be satisfied with a little improvement in attendance when special days can be converted into something sensational? Days like these offer ready-made opportunities for doing something extra and unusual, especially in regard to attendance.

What makes a day memorable? What sends worshipers home saying to others, "Oh, you should have been at church this morning?" Special music, participation in the service by members of the congregation and community, an atmosphere of something exciting and innovative can all help to make the day remembered; it just takes preparation and planning.

One secret for success in any effort for improved attendance is to involve as many individuals and organizations as possible. Use all your musical talent. Appoint committees. Send special invitations to organizations that would have reason to be interested. Invite local dignitaries.

Mother's Day, for example, ought to be a time when the whole family is at church to honor mother. Flowers or corsages can be provided for every woman who is present, recognizing them as mothers or as potential mothers. Men attending the service can be given a colored flower as a boutonniere if they have a living mother or a white flower if their mother has passed on. Mothers should be honored during the service, perhaps by calling attention to the oldest mother present as well as the youngest mother. Remember, everybody has a mother, and this special day can involve everyone. Some may decry such a service as sentimental, but there are times and places for such things and Mother's Day is one of them.

If it does not give offense to others, choose a "Mother of the Year." This can be someone who has a distinguished record in home, church, and community. Then be sure to exploit this honor with news and photos for the local press and television. Plan to present a document, plaque, or bouquet. And then why not invite the mayor or some other respected local official to make the presentation?

Thanksgiving also offers a special opportunity for involvement of people. Contributions of foodstuffs,

9

canned goods, and the like for institutions of the church or for the other charitable purposes can be a highlight of the service. Special thanks for benefits received during the year ought to be voiced clearly, perhaps by asking each worshiper to write on a piece of paper one thing for which that person is especially grateful. Then have these papers collected by the ushers and placed on the altar. Some persons may be willing to stand up and express their thanks vocally, but there are many who would be embarrassed to do this and others who might not know when to stop. It's important never to make anyone feel uncomfortable.

Since Thanksgiving is a community festival, it's a time to invite organizations such as 4-H clubs, conservationists, civic groups, or patriotic societies to take part (see sample).

Days of confirmation or baptism ought to be a reminder to all members of their own commitment, whenever or wherever it was made. They can join in a restatement of their own vows rather than simply be spectators at someone else's.

Every event of this sort has the potential for being a big day in the life of your church. But all your planning and preparation won't work unless people know that something special is to take place and are stimulated to attend and take part in it. By sending out a postcard you can let people know that it's to be a special day. Whatever other publicity network you have should be used fully. Advance articles sent to local news outlets, and even paid advertising can help a somewhat unusual event become a time for excitement and festivity in the congregation. Make it work and people will go home saying to others, "Oh, you should have been at church today!"

BICENTENNIAL THANKSGIVING DAY FESTIVAL

NOVEMBER 27   10:00 A.M.

Harvest Home Display
Bicentennial Opening
Sermon, "Goodness Never Fails"

First Church

Grant Street, Downtown Pittsburgh

2.

Fabricate a Festival!

Some communities have become well known because they hold an annual festival which attracts national attention. Thousands come to Kutztown, Pennsylvania, for example, for its Pennsylvania Dutch Days. Vermont communities have a Fall Foliage Festival, New Jersey shore towns, a seafood festival, and a small Kansas community draws throngs for its Swedish folk festival. Look at some others:

Mobile, Ala.—Azalea Trail Festival
Homestead, Fla.—Frontier Days
Biloxi, Miss.—Shrimp Festival
Savannah, Ga.—Arts Festival
Charleston, S.C.—Spoleto Festival

Ever wonder why these communities attach so much importance to these festivals? They bring people into the community, awaken community spirit, gain great publicity for the community, and, more than incidentally, make money. Whether based on ethnic heritage, local customs, or some historic event, such programs have great commercial and publicity value. Why can't the children of light, in this case, be as wise as the children of this world? Why can't your church create a festival to reap these same benefits?

Festivals are by their very nature times of joy and celebration. Long before secular festivals like those listed above were important to communities, the great religious festivals such as Christmas, Easter, and Pentecost were highlights of the year for every church. But why stop there?

In each congregation or parish there's at least one unique day or event that deserves special celebration. It may simply be "Founder's Day," or the day that is

dedicated to the source of the church's name—St. Mark's Day or Wesley's birthday or whatever. In every case, there's an annual birthday anniversary that could be converted into something memorable. Everyone has a birthday every year, and every institution has an anniversary every year. Why not capitalize on them?

The procedure can be very much like that of celebrating the special "small festivals" mentioned in the preceding chapter. However, fabricating a festival requires the development of one or two unique factors that can be continued year after year with effectiveness. They'll become traditions, in time. One church bulletin announced that "This year we are instituting the tradition of an Easter breakfast." Well, traditions are handed down from generation to generation, not "instituted." The Easter breakfast may indeed have established iself as a tradition after a period of years of successful operation, but it didn't start out that way!

A tradition has to start out somehow. How do you find the uniqueness needed to make your festival something special? One Pennsylvania congregation celebrates its festival each June with the presentation of one red rose to a descendant of the colonial landowners who gave the ground on which to build its first church building. "One red rose forever" was the rent exacted by Baron Spiegel from the Lutheran congregation at Manheim, Pennsylvania, and the "payment" of this rent has been resurrected in recent years as a major community festival.

Rural congregations have found that a summertime reunion of families related to the congregation makes a great community program. People who have moved far away are drawn back by the event. In the town of Plains, Georgia, which has been mentioned in the news frequently because it is the home of a president, a Lutheran congregation holds such a summertime reunion for all relatives and descendants of the families that first established the congregation early in the 1800s. Since Rosalyn Carter, wife of President Jimmy Carter, comes from one of these families, the presence of the President's family and its inevitable entourage has drawn the national spotlight to this observance.

One feature of any "fabricated" festival ought to be a memento—maybe just a spray of wheat, if it's a Harvest Festival in mid-America, or a seashell, if it's an event in a coastal area. It can be a flower or a commemorative booklet. People value such trophies, and they serve as reminders of the event.

Alert congregations will also find ways to obtain the names and addresses of people participating. This can be done by asking them to sign up for a souvenir to be mailed at a later date—a photograph or the news report of the festival, for example. When that mailing goes out, an offering envelope can be enclosed and this is almost sure to bring in more than enough to pay for the mailing! The names and addresses can also be the basis for a mailing list for announcements of similar affairs and of the same event on subsequent years. The list will also provide a roster of friends of the congregation who may be called upon for help in time of need. The festival itself, however, should not be primarily a money-raising affair.

Let's add again that the success of any program like this depends on two factors—people and publicity. Don't let a small committee carry the whole burden, and don't hide your light under a bushel! Appoint special committees for the program, the memento, the hospitality, for gathering names of those present, for publicity, and for refreshments or other social activity that accompanies the festival. Then in your advance publicity, release the names of committee members to the press, *one committee at a time*. In this way, you'll get five or six brief mentions in the newspaper, a much more likely possibility than one big feature article. By involving a large number of individuals and by aggressive use of publicity, you're sure of a large attendance, and a large attendance ensures the success of your festival.

3.

No More "Low Sunday"

In the Episcopal Church the liturgical calendar lists the Sunday after Easter as "Low Sunday." There's a standing joke (and not only among Episcopalians) that the designation refers to the attendance. In many churches, after the strenuous Easter week the minister thinks he or she deserves a vacation, the choir likewise, and the congregation therefore feels free to take the day off as well.

To some degree, this happened in my parish. Then one Easter Sunday I told the congregation that Easter isn't the end of anything, but rather the beginning. "If Easter has any meaning in your life, you will make it a beginning of a new season of worship and praise!" I announced that the following Sunday we would have another Easter service, an Easter Afterglow, and that we would expect each worshiper to whom Easter meant anything to be present.

Would it work? Well, it did, but it took careful advance preparation. For one thing, we had a volunteer choir that was always augmented by a half-dozen good voices for the Easter services. Some of them quipped that by joining the choir for Easter they were assured of getting a good seat in church. The result was that Easter music was always good and that the remnant of the choir that returned for the Sunday after Easter was a decided letdown.

It was essential to get a commitment from the choir members if the Easter Afterglow was to work. I asked all the Easter singers to promise that they would return and again sing the joyous Easter anthems on the following Sunday. One or two were unable to promise because of other engagements, but enough responded to provide us with a highly acceptable choir.

Others in the congregation became enthusiastic about the idea. We did not attempt to equal the display of Easter flowers in the chancel, but we had a tasteful tribute of spring flowers.

```
E A S T E R      A F T E R G L O W      S E R V I C E S
---------      ------------------      ---------------

       SUNDAY   APRIL  14  at  8  AND 11 O'Clock

                 ST. PAUL'S CHURCH
        Church St. and Longfellow Ave., Teaneck, N.J.

EASTER MUSIC --- EASTER MESSAGE ---- EASTER  HYMNS


    EASTER marks the beginning of a new and risen life
with the RISEN CHRIST!  If EASTER means anything in
your life, come and worship with us this Sunday!
And bring your family and friends!
    Your RISEN LORD calls you to worship and we are
expecting you to be with us.

                                   Pastor
```

On Easter Monday a postcard was sent to all members of the congregation urging their attendance at the Easter Afterglow service (see sample). "Easter hymns—Easter music—Easter message," it proclaimed. Only the postcard and our regular newspaper ad were used for promotion.

Results were not spectacular, but they were encouraging enough to continue the plan for several years. Anytime you can nearly double your normal attendance, you're doing all right! After a few years, as always happens, the novelty began to wear off, and we gave it a rest for a while. But by that time, the congregation had grown, and faithful attendance kept the averages high throughout the year.

Below are our actual church attendance figures for Easter Sunday and for the Sunday after Easter over a six-year span. Can you guess on which four of these six years we had the Easter Afterglow emphasis?

	Easter Sunday	Sunday after Easter
Year 1	527	123
Year 2	535	215
Year 3	642	245
Year 4	609	237
Year 5	682	214
Year 6	647	170

4.

Invite the City

In your neighborhood there are probably other churches, not too different from yours, with similar aims, goals, and problems. While there are often valid differences that keep churches apart, particularly in doctrine and worship, there are also times when the needs of the community demand that they work together. A time of national emergency, a disaster of some sort, or even a great community social program provide a basis for such interchurch cooperation. A show of unity among churches always makes a deep impact on a community.

When churches work together, one of them naturally becomes the leader, and the others look to it for guidance. Why shouldn't your church be the one to lead?

Unless you have some strict doctrinal reason for building a wall around your church, look across the way to the other churches of your area. Are there congregations whose cooperation would strengthen the causes for which you are striving? Could you all cooperate in so simple a program as a community go-to-church Sunday (or weekend, if Seventh-Day Adventists are involved)?

Something like this happened in the Pocono Mountains of Pennsylvania with a greater degree of success than anyone had dared anticipate. A group of churches got together to organize a tremendous media campaign with a go-to-church theme, using newspapers and radio to call the whole community to worship. An impact was made not only on the community, but on the churches themselves. Some of them found for the first time that they could plan and complete a major project. The program opened the doors for further cooperation. Best of all, it heightened the recognition factor for the churches involved. For many of them, it marked the first time they had had an important influence on their community.

AN INVITATION FROM YOUR LOCAL CHURCH

We're asking you to come to church this Sunday and judge for yourself if face-to-face religion can give you a happier, more meaningful Monday . . .

*and Tuesday
and Wednesday
and Thursday
and Friday
and Saturday.*

APPENZELL—ST. MARKS Off Rt. 715, 11 A.M.	**MINISINK HILLS—ST. MARKS** 10 A.M., 629-0358
BRODHEADSVILLE—ZION Rt. 209 10:30 A.M., 992-4517	**MT. POCONO—OUR SAVIOUR'S** 675 Belmont Ave., 8:30 & 11 A.M., 839-8121
EAST STROUDSBURG—GRACE 25 Lackawanna Ave. 8:30 & 11 A.M., 421-6511	**SCOTRUN—ST. JOHN'S** Off Rt. 611, 9 A.M.
HAMILTON SQUARE—CHRIST 10:30 A.M. 992-6601	**STONE CHURCH, PA.—CHRIST** Rt. 611, 10:30 A.M., 215-588-3056
KRESGEVILLE—SALEM-ST. PAULS Rt. 209, 9:30 A.M., 215-681-5517	**STROUDSBURG—ST. JOHN'S** 9th St., 9 & 11 A.M., 421-8520
MARSHALLS CREEK—ST. PAUL'S Rt. 209, 8:30 & 11 A.M., 421-5644	**TANNERSVILLE—ST. PAULS** 9:30 & 11 A.M., 629-1773

Newspaper advertising prepared for the "come to church" project in the Pocono region of Pennsylvania can be adapted to any similar local or regional program.

An Invitation From
Your Local Church

We're asking you to come to church this Sunday and judge for yourself if face-to-face religion can give you a happier, more meaningful Monday . . .

*and Tuesday
and Wednesday
and Thursday
and Friday
and Saturday.*

APPENZELL
St. Mark's—Off Rt.715
11:00 A.M.

BRODHEADSVILLE
Zion—Rt. 209
10:30 A.M., 992-4517

EAST STROUDSBURG
Grace—25 Lackawanna Ave.
near Analomink St.
8:30 & 11:00, 421-6511

HAMILTON SQUARE
Christ
10:30 A.M., 992-6601

KRESGEVILLE
Salem-St. Paul's—Route 209
9:30 A.M., 215-681-5517

MARSHALLS CREEK
St. Paul's—1 mi. S. of Marshalls Creek
Business Rt. 209
8:30 & 11:00 A.M., 421-5644

MINISINK HILLS
St.Mark's—River Road
10:00 A.M., 629-0358

MT. POCONO
Our Savior's—LC/MS
675 Belmont Ave.
8:30 & 11:00 A.M., 839-8121

SCOTRUN
St. John's—Off Rt. 611
9:00 A.M.

STONE CHURCH, PA.
Christ—Route 611
10:30 A.M., 215-588-3056

STROUDSBURG
St. John's—9th St. near Main
9:00 & 11:00 A.M., 421-8520

TANNERSVILLE
St. Paul's—Rt. 611 South of Rt. 715
9:30 & 11:00 A.M.
629-1773

The advice given to congregations participating in the "media blitz" in the Pocono region of Pennsylvania makes an excellent check list that applies to congregations everywhere.

CONGREGATIONAL FOLLOW-UP FOR VISITORS
RESULTING FROM MEDIA BLITZ

YOU'VE GOT TO BE READY OR YOU'LL MISS THE BOAT

THE RECEPTION OF THE VISITOR

THE GREETERS
It is important to have greeters at the door ready to welcome and identify all visitors resulting from the Media Blitz. No one can go unnoticed.

PASTOR'S GREETING
It is important that the pastor greet visitors from the Media Blitz, recognize them as such, and identify them and offer his personal services, and offer to make a visitation if desired.

ALL THE CONGREGATION
All members of the congregation must be alerted to the possibility of extra visitors during the period of the Media Blitz and required to make them feel welcome by greeting visitors, introducing themselves, and extending an invitation to return.

THE PASTOR AND THE SERVICE

PASTOR'S APPEARANCE
Is your pastor carefully groomed and dressed? Does he have a general appearance that is acceptable to you, and makes you proud to say: "This is my pastor?"

SERMON CONTENT
If promotion brings people into the church, and the sermon does not attract and hold them, the promotion is futile.

CONDUCT OF SERVICES
Services should be worshipful, in good order and taste, and start and end on time in a temperature conducive to a worshipful atmosphere.

MUSIC
Music should be familiar, with good leadership from the organ and choir. New hymns should be taught, not sprung.

CHOIR DEPORTMENT
The choir should be robed and unobtrusive. They are there to lead congregational singing and to render anthems, not to put on a show for the members.

SUNDAY BULLETINS
The bulletin should contain clear directions for the conduct of the service, and *all* announcements for the day. The service should not regularly be interrupted for announcements.

THE PLANT

CHURCH SIGNS
Did you ever drive past your church at the legal speed limit and see if you could identify the building from the sign out front? If you can't, you need help. Is your sign an attractive addition to the architecture or an eye-sore?

PARKING LOT
You're no different than a shopping mall. You should have more parking places than are normally needed. If you're short of stalls in the parking lot, you may be short of people in the pews.

CLEAN SIDEWALKS
What's the first impression you get from your church when you approach? Are the sidewalks clean? The grass cut? Does it look like somebody cares? I'm coming to church looking for people who care. Is the first impression of your church, "they care?"

CLEAN CHURCH BUILDING
If you invite me to your home, I expect you and your home to be prepared to receive me. If your church building is not clean and inviting, I'm going to leave with a bad impression, and I'm not coming back.

As every corporate advertiser knows, there's great psychological value just in making prospective customers aware of your existence. In the case of churches, there's a similar lasting value. Afterward, if a visitor calls on some mission and says, "Hi, I'm from First Church," the residual recognition factor from the campaign may make further explanation needless. First Church is *known* in the community.

The Pocono program utilized a "Face to Face Religion" campaign developed by the Lutheran Church in America. The material called for a media saturation effort, including paid advertising in the newspapers and on the radio. The procedure covered a four-week period, stressing the go-to-church-on-Sunday message. Through repetition and the use of a single simple appeal, it was hoped that the idea would filter into the consciousness of every person living in the area. Similar campaigns among Lutheran churches in Iowa and Ohio had proved effective. For example, in an Ohio city, despite a record-breaking cold wave, attendance figures at the Sunday services for the campaign weekend averaged 60 percent above those of the previous year.

About three months before the proposed start of the Pocono campaign, pastors of ten churches were called together for a luncheon meeting. Here's where the influence of the "leader church" is important. Those attending the luncheon were given a preview of the kind of advertising material planned for newspapers and radio, along with a briefing on the requirements for each participating congregation. The congregations had a total membership of 2,807, and the initial request was for a contribution of $1 per member, which would provide for the radio time and newspaper space that would be purchased. All the congregations agreed to participate, but as expected not all of them paid their full share of the costs. It was still possible during the four-week "media blitz" to have a one-eighth-page newspaper ad each Monday and Wednesday and a quarter-page ad each Friday. The newspaper ads were vital to the program, since they listed all the participating churches and their hours of service. Although 40 radio spots of 30 seconds each were programmed each week, their brevity didn't permit the use of such details.

One month before the media blitz, a full program outline was sent to each church. Each was urged to play up the program in its bulletins, parish newsletters, and pulpit announcements. Weekly letters were thereafter sent to each church with up-to-the-minute information. Anticipating that a large number of visitors and some strangers would be coming to the churches as a result of the campaign, the committee in charge prepared a comprehensive set of instructions for congregations, telling them, "You've got to be ready or you'll miss the boat." These instructions are so essential for any congregation that they're sampled here.

The Pocono event was sufficiently successful that the congregations willingly agreed upon a similar event the following December, which they dubbed the "Christmas Blitz." It consisted of a three-day, pre-Christmas church attendance campaign. Since Christmas fell on a Sunday, the "Christmas Blitz" used twelve 30-second radio commercials on Thursday and Friday, followed by a full-page newspaper ad on Saturday. The ad included Christmas greetings, plus the listing of Christmas Eve and Christmas Day services at each of the churches.

A similar campaign in your area would call first for someone to contact all churches likely to be interested. If there's a local council or a ministerial association, this would be the natural starting point. If no such ecumenical organization exists or if your church is not part of it, some individual must start things off by inviting representatives of interested churches to a meeting at which a program is outlined. Those participating should be urged to provide input for the program. Some may have special contacts with the media.

The next step is to set up a general committee with power to take action. Committee members must then personally contact the radio stations and newspapers, offering to buy space or time but requesting editorial support and favorable treatment on rates. Since this is a newsworthy undertaking, it should merit generous mention in news columns and on news broadcasts.

Once costs are ascertained, participating churches should be asked to pay their fair share in advance. Cash in advance is always helpful because there's likely to be some group that tries to wiggle out of paying with some flimsy excuse. Not all Christians bear one another's burdens, and some don't even bear their own burdens! In setting up the budget, try to keep it as low as possible. The program should not run the risk of falling into debt.

After this preliminary work, it's important for someone to coordinate the program by keeping in close touch with all the churches. Each congregation should use its own resources of talent to strengthen the program, giving it added publicity through their own channels.

This program works. It produces a big surge in church attendance, if only because church members themselves will turn out to see what's happening. It establishes an important recognition factor in the community for all the participating churches. It awakens the whole community to the moral leadership of the churches. It just takes someone to spark it. Why shouldn't your church be the leader in your area?

5.
Never the Twain Shall Meet

If you have more than one service on a Sunday morning, you'll eventually have a problem. People will get settled into the habit of attending one of the services, thus forming congregational groups which are separate from each other. When this happens, your problem has arrived. How can it be solved in order to achieve a unified congregation rather than two which feel they are strangers to each other?

One possibility, if the services are separated by a Sunday school hour, is to cancel the Sunday school sessions occasionally and substitute a family-unity hour. Those attending the early service are asked to remain for an extra hour, while those attending the later service are asked to come early. The interim period is a fun session of song, story, and simple games that have people mingle a bit and get acquainted with one another. There's always room for a serious moment, too, in order to describe some of the congregation's aims and goals and stir up enthusiasm for their achievement.

Another possibility for unity exists when congregations have a church picnic. Name cards for all those who attend will help introduce people to each other. If there's a sit-down lunch or dinner, suggest that early-service people and late-service people sit next to one another. This ought to be done at congregational dinners, also. Too often, no public recognition is given to the fact that there are really two different congregations and that they don't know one another as well as they might. By openly admitting the problem and having some fun with it, a congregation can make its job of promotion, stewardship, and evangelism very much easier since visitors are then not calling on a stranger but rather on someone they know.

Congregations that have two or more services must make a conscious effort to persuade their people to intermingle. It's an effort that pays.

6.

Plan the Whole Year

Don't you sometimes get tired of having events sneak up on you, finding you unprepared? Nobody likes uncertainty, and all too often the days slip by faster than we expect. Then some anniversary or festival looms right in front of us, leaving far too little time for us to make the proper preparations.

After dealing with this kind of problem frequently, we decided to hold a "planning day" on which all the organizations and committees of the church would meet briefly to outline what meetings and events they planned to have during the year. Then we would make a comprehensive list of all the activities, putting them all together into one coordinated, whole-year program. When the committees and organizations had completed their presentations, the church council reviewed the proposals. Some had to be vetoed because of conflicts or because of costs. But after these had been removed, the rest presented a complete picture of what we'd be doing during the year ahead. Of course, emergencies might arise to interfere with some plans, but that's a fact of life anyway.

Included in this comprehensive program were special worship opportunities, since the pastors had been expected to provide input along with the organizations! Musical events and all other worship-related matters were also included, lest they be overshadowed by some event of lesser importance. Then we got into the weekday evening events—regular meetings, special meetings, dinners, and various programs. By the time the list was finished there weren't many vacant spots!

A glance through the list indicates its completeness—every date when Holy Communion was to be offered, the times of meeting for the pastor's class, special occasions like the Father-and-Son Banquet,

Youth Banquet, or Mother-and-Daughter Banquet, Usher's Acknowledgment Dinner, congregational dinners and meetings, prayer breakfasts, and fellowship events. Included also were notations about special worship days—Thanksgiving, Christmas, Epiphany, Lent, Pentecost. Even such minor things as the days when coffee fellowship took place between the services (we had two services each Sunday morning, and this was one means of getting the two worshiping communities to meet together) or after-church receptions were on the list.

Members of the congregation responded eagerly to the resulting list. People said to us over and over again, "This is really great because now I can make my own plans. Before we make dinner dates or arrange outings, we can check and make sure we won't be missing something important at church." We urged people to take the list home and to mark their own calendars, indicating what events they planned to attend so that under no circumstances would other things come along and interfere. We hoped in that way to avoid some of the conflicts which all too often occur between church events and secular affairs, such as school programs, civic affairs, or cultural activities.

The list was also a help to the church staff, giving them the advantage of knowing well in advance what their obligations would be. For leaders like the church council, it was an eye-opener as to what the church's program really included and how extensive it was. An outsider might view the large number of dinners and comment that we were sure eager to eat, but in our own situation we found that people had to come to the church from long distances throughout the entire metropolitan area and that one of the best arrangements to get them together was to include a meal. If

Planning ahead can show you where your calendar is too full or too empty. Here's one month's activity at St. Mark Church, Dunedin, Florida. How does yours compare?

February 1979

	SUNDAY	MONDAY	TUESDAY	WEDNESDAY	THURSDAY	FRIDAY	SATURDAY
					1 8:30 Staff Meeting 10:00 Anna Akers Pr., Grp. 1:30 Prayer Group Leaders 5-7:00 Movin' & Groovin' 7-8:00 Choir 8:15-9:45 "2,7" Series-#3 Loeffler – 6th gr. classroom 8:15-9:45 "2,7" Series-#2 Skeddenbenz-Lounge	**2** 8:30 Altar Guild – Work Session 10:00 Intercessory Prayer	**3** 9-10:00 Confirmation Class 5:00 Worship Service
4 HOLY COMMUNION Worship 8:30 & 11:00 Sermon: "A Calling of Voices" Hymns: 131, 374, 285 Church School 9:40	**5** 9:30-11:30 St. Mark Women	**6** 10:50 A 10:00 Anna Akers Pr., Grp. 10:00 "2,7" Series – #2 at Judie Elgin's home 5-7:00 Movin' & Groovin 7:30 Curlew City Loeffler – 6th gr. class, Skeddenbenz–#2-Lounge	**7** 9:30-11:00 "2,7" Series Loeffler – 6th gr. classroom Prayer Group Leaders 10:00 Manon Fresh 10:50 Sue Bakke 7:00 Prayer & Praise	**8** 10:00 Intercessory Prayer	**9** 9-10:00 Confirmation Class 9-3:30 Prayer Workshop– Bradenton – Bring Sack Lunch	**10** 6:00 Curlew Zone Meeting– Social Hall 5:00 Worship Service
11 Worship 8:30 & 11:00 Sermon: "Victory in Praise" Hymns: 557, 429, 408 Church School 9:40 7:00 Library Guild	**12** Prayer Group Leaders 10:00 Betty Fresh 10:00 Mildred Ward 10:00 Ann Zuffa 10:00 Peg Rundquist 10:00 Lucille Skari-Lounge 3:00 Jane Farley	**13** 3:00 Altar Guild – Study Session 4:30-5:10 Cherub Choir	**14** 8:30 Staff Meeting 9:30-11:00 "2,7" Series Loeffler – 6th gr. classm. Prayer Group Leaders 10:00 Manon Fresh 10:50 Sue Bakke 7:00 Prayer & Praise	**15** 10:00 Anna Akers Pr., Grp. 10:00 "2,7" Series-Elgin's 1-2:00 Voter Registration 5-7:00 Movin' & Groovin' 7-8:00 Choir 8:15-9:45 "2,7" Series– Loeffler–6th gr. classm. Skeddenbenz-#2-Lounge	**16** 10:00 Intercessory Prayer	**17** 9-10:00 Confirmation Class 5:00 Worship Service
18 Worship 8:30 & 11:00 Sermon: "Growing Thru Adversity" Hymns: 172, 516, 385 Church School 9:40 6:30-8:00 Youth Ministry to visit Juvenile Detention Home	**19** Prayer Group Leaders 10:00 Betty Fresh 10:00 Mildred Ward 10:00 Ann Zuffa 10:00 Peg Rundquist 10:00 Lucille Skari-Lounge 3:00 Jane Farley 7:30 Nurses' Ministry	**20** 4:30-5:10 Cherub Choir 6:00 Covered Dish Dinner Curlew Zone, Hosts 10:00 Sue Bakke	**21** 9:30-11:00 "2,7" Ser. Loeffler–6th gr. classroom Prayer Group Leaders 10:00 "2,7" Series-Elgin's Judie Elgin's home 7-8:00 Choir 8:15-9:45 "2,7" Series – Loeffler–6th gr. classm.	**22** 10:00 Anna Akers Pr., Grp. 10:00 "2,7" Series – #2 – 5-7:00 Movin' & Groovin"	**23** 10:00 Intercessory Prayer	**24** 9-10:00 Confirmation Class 5:00 Worship Service
25 Worship 8:30 & 11:00 Sermon: "Transfiguration" Hymns: 438, 474, 481 Church School 9:40 6:30-8:00 Youth Ministry "2,7" Series–Course #2 Reception of New Members	**26** Prayer Group Leaders 10:00 Betty Fresh 10:00 Mildred Ward 10:00 Ann Zuffa 10:00 Peg Rundquist 10:00 Lucille Skari-Lounge 3:00 Jane Farley Devotional Books Begin	**26** 9:30-1:00 Christian Service Day 1:00 St. Mark Women – Board Meeting – Lounge 4:30-5:10 Cherub Choir	**27** 9:30-11:00 "2,7" Series Prayer Group Leaders 10:00 Manon Fresh 10:00 Sue Bakke 7:30 Sunday Sch. Teacher Workshop on Prayer in the Classroom 7:00 Prayer & Praise	**28**		

2:00 Youth Ministry to visit Juvenile Detention Home

6:30 Church Council and Zone Officers Buffet Dinner and Meeting – Social Hall they had to go home from work, prepare and eat dinner (and clean up), and then start out for church, it would have posed great difficulties for many of them. By making it a full evening at church, including dinner, their arrangements were simplified.

Try it in your church. When you plot out the entire year, the gaps in your program become obvious. Where necessary, you can persuade groups to reschedule some events so they don't conflict with others. You can see ahead to the periods when you're going to be rushed with time-consuming affairs and can therefore plan adequately. On the other hand, if there are open spaces in the year's program, you'll know that you've found a good time for scheduling new activities. Overall, it will help you and your people to get a general view of the church's program and to evaluate how well it is serving their needs.

7.

Cottage Meetings

Your members may sometimes feel isolated. "Nobody from my neighborhood belongs to our church," they'll say. "Wouldn't it be nice if we could share rides to church or if our children could go to classes together."

The simple fact is that many members don't know where other members live. They meet at church services or at organizations, but rarely in one another's houses. Cottage meetings, or neighborhood meetings, can help overcome this problem. The idea isn't new, as the very term "cottage meeting" indicates. The term probably comes from the early days of the industrial revolution, when some manufacturers did not have factories as central places for manufacture, but gave workers piecework to take home. When the work was completed, the workers brought it back to the manufacturer and usually got paid very little for it. Out of this came the term "cottage industry" or "sweat system," usually in reference to cheap labor.

Meeting in the homes of members can be helpful. Many congregations hold their first services in the homes of members or potential members, until they can find a central meeting place. In some congrega-tions, prayer circles or Bible study groups meet in the homes of members.

To prepare for a congregation-wide cottage meet-ing plan, the first step is to adopt some specific purpose or goal for the meetings. In one congrega-tion, local conditions made some members timid about traveling at night to services or other events at the church. They felt secure in their own neighbor-hoods, however, so a series of neighborhood cottage meetings was set up. In another case, an effort to save gasoline by shortening the amount of travel necessary led to the adoption of cottage meetings rather than weeknight travel to the more-distant church building. Still another case, described in detail below, was a one-shot cottage meeting program set up to stimulate Lenten attendance.

Whatever the underlying purpose of the cottage meetings, the universal effect of them is to acquaint members in neighborhoods with other members who are their neighbors. You'll be surprised how many times people will come to such a meeting, spot some acquaintance, and say, "Why, I never knew you lived in this neighborhood." It's also an opportunity for the minister or for church leaders to meet with small group of members to discuss church programs, perhaps simply as a by-product of the main purpose of the meeting.

The first step in setting up a congregation-wide series of cottage meetings is to divide the congregation into neighborhood groups of no more than twenty persons. A number larger than this is difficult to accommodate in the average home and places an unfair load on the host. It also takes away some of the desired intimacy.

The second step is to find within each group a chairperson (preferably a volunteer) who will call the people in the group and invite them to his or her home for an evening. The chairperson is also the leader for the group, to as great a degree as possible. Adequate materials and training must be provided for these leaders to assure that the group meetings are effective, since the minister can probably not attend all the sessions. To get the most out of the group meeting, the program should be limited to one hour, leaving at least another hour for sociability and refreshments.

With a personal invitation from a neighbor, the attendance at such group meetings is good. About fifteen of the twenty persons invited can be expected to show up. It's therefore a way of personally making contact with about 75 percent of the congregation's membership in a relatively easy and informal manner. This should appeal to ministers.

One congregation set up cottage meetings as a prelude to the Lenten season. Ten meetings were scheduled in various parts of the parish, with no more than two being held on the same night. This made it possible for the pastor to attend and to address each group briefly. When he had two groups in the same night, one group held its devotional period and heard his address first, with refreshments following. The second group started off with a social hour, delaying its devotional period until the time of the pastor's arrival. While this meant busy evenings for the pastor

for two full weeks, it also gave him a coveted opportunity to meet personally in a home atmosphere with hundreds of church members. It paid!

A Pittsburgh congregation with a widely scattered membership also set up this kind of pre-Lenten cottage meeting. The chairperson of each meeting was provided with a brochure outlining the congregation's entire Lenten program, including church services, fellowship events, and other worship opportunities. The arrangement enabled the congregation to get its message directly to about 75 percent of the membership, an achievement in itself. But it also provided an incentive for those attending to follow up the cottage meetings by attendance at church services during the following weeks. To ensure this, an attendance record was kept at the services with each member asked to register attendance at church. Absence on one Sunday was noted by a postcard sent to the member saying that he or she was missed. Absence on two Sundays led to a phone call from either the neighborhood chairperson or from a member of the church's staff. Three Sundays absence led to a personal visit from one of the church staff. (For a plan that makes attendance-taking easy, see chapter 13.)

Usually, by the time a personal visit is made, Lent is half over. Since Lenten attendance usually starts slowly and builds up as Easter approaches, the pre-Lenten survey was a reversal of the usual trend and enabled the season to start off with a bang.

The attendance survey wasn't always appreciated. Some people thought the whole thing was ridiculous and simply did not fill out the attendance card. Then they got very irritated when they got a postcard, then a phone call, and finally a visit because they had been in church but had not filled out the attendance card. Our standard answer to them was, "Well, at least you know we care." Many of them were impressed with the fact that we really did care!

8.
A People's Service

Unless you are locked into an inflexible liturgy, you probably adapt your order for worship to different times and seasons. This takes planning, and inevitably the service reflects the tastes and choices of the minister or the worship committee. But your people are likely to be saying, "Hey, we have favorites, too. Why can't we make the selections once in a while?"

Whether you do it once a month, quarterly, or even only once a year, why not give members a chance to make the decisions? You can't do this during the service by simply asking, "Anybody got a special hymn they'd like us to sing?" Then the person who shouts the loudest probably makes the selection and 90 percent of the congregation may not be in agreement with the choice.

The way to do it is to announce well in advance that you will hold a request day. Hand out forms or blank sheets to your members, asking them to list four or five of their favorite hymns with the promise that on the appointed day the congregation will sing the four hymns that got the top votes from the congregation. You can be sure that they'll all turn out in anticipation of singing "my hymn."

Along with this, ask the people to select the sermon theme for the day, not just by choosing some old sermon they happen to remember, but rather by indicating the topic they feel needs most to be treated from the pulpit. Warning to preachers: you may be shocked and surprised by their choice!

If you're really daring you can go a step farther and ask members of the congregation to select their favorite anthem for rendition by the choir. The problem here is that the selection may not be within the capability of the choir, or it may be some far-out rock and roll song which you wouldn't want sung in church. However, a compromise method in this regard would be to ask the choir members to vote for their favorite anthem and then have them sing it. When they like an anthem, choir members are likely to sing it exceptionally well.

By following this simple procedure, you can allow the congregation to plan its own service. For those in the congregation who seem always to find fault with the selection of the hymns or with some other facet of the service, this reduces their cause for complaint. At least a few times during the year, you can say to the people, "This is exactly what the majority of you want. You've picked the hymns, the sermon topic, and maybe the anthem, so we'll all enjoy it together."

9.
People Love to Sing

People love to sing, but not everybody can. In one small country church in New Jersey, the leading member was a deaf septuagenarian. At every service he sat in the back row and bellowed out the hymns off-key with a voice that drowned out the wheezy reed organ. Singing in that congregation was somewhat below par. At the other end of the scale, there are affluent urban and suburban congregations that employ excellent paid choirs. The choirs do all the singing. Members of the congregation seem to feel, "We're paying the choir to sing, so why should we do it?"

Your congregation probably falls between these two extremes. You feel music is an integral part of Christian worship and that it should not be limited to a few. The problem is how to get everybody to sing, and how to help them enjoy doing it.

We felt that one reason some people didn't enjoy singing was that the hymns were unfamiliar to them. At social gatherings, these same people might delight in roaring out a rendition of "Down by the Old Mill Stream." But in church their lips were buttoned up, especially on new hymns. If we sang only the dozen or so hackneyed old favorites, they might participate. But not on new hymns.

One Sunday we decided to try something different.

Instead of starting the service at the appointed hour, we announced that since a new and relatively unknown hymn had been chosen as one of those we were to sing, we'd have a brief practice period to enable everybody in the congregation to join in the singing. Since this was an unexpected move, it got good attention from the congregation. Those people who hated new hymns were already in the pews and couldn't very well leave. We had a captive audience.

The pastor began by telling a little about the new hymn—who wrote it, what its message was, why it was included in the hymnal. Then he led the congregation in reading the words, so that each person might understand their meaning. The organist then played through the hymn two times, after which the choir leader took over. First the choir sang the hymn one line at a time, with the choir leader pointing out the musical accents. Then we hummed along for a verse while the choir sang it. Finally the whole congregation joined in singing.

The whole process took about ten minutes. When the hymn came along in the course of the service, people sang it well. It was no longer new and unfamiliar. And many of them said, "Why don't we do this every time we have a new hymn?"

10.

Hold a Wedding Reunion

How many couples have been married in your church? If you check back over a period of years, you may be surprised to find how many of them have since moved away. In our mobile age, many young people get married in their home church or in the church of the bride, only to move away immediately to start their life together in some distant place.

After fifteen years in my parish I found that I had officiated at the weddings of more than three hundred couples! Not all were church weddings, of course, but all were under the auspices of the church in some way. Only a small percentage of the couples were still in our area. Some had simply disappeared, and we had no way to discover their present whereabouts.

As part of an anniversary celebration, it seemed good to hold a wedding reunion service at which all those who had plighted their troth at the church or under its auspices would be invited to attend. Invitations that looked like typical wedding invitations were therefore sent to all whose addresses we could find. Where the church records no longer contained the addresses, we generally found that relatives or friends were able to provide them for us. We actually invited more than two hundred of the couples, and when the service was held we had about one hundred of the couples in attendance. Of the others, many lived too far away to make the trip.

The sermon was about the Christian home. The music included some of the old wedding favorites, like "O Perfect Love" and "Lord, Who at Cana's Wedding Feast." The Scripture readings were those used at the marriage service. Rather than ask the couples to stand and repeat their vows before the altar, which might have been embarrassing for some, we decided to add a light touch by saying that since the bride and groom are often in such a daze that they don't know what's happening, we'd all join in reading and repeating the words.

The wedding reunion was a great success. A service of this kind cannot be repeated too frequently, of course. A reasonable interval—perhaps as much as five years—ought to elapse between wedding reunion services. But there are variations. Why not try a reunion of all those who were among the charter members of your congregation, if it was recently organized? Or if it was organized many years ago, the reunion could bring together those who had been members for 50 years or more. As a social event, we had an occasional reunion of all former members of the church council, usually in connection with a meeting of the present council. There are many variations on this theme, and they're all worth a try.

11.
Break the Record!

Playing the numbers game is not good if it's done just to boast about the crowds that throng your temple. Jesus preached to and taught thousands at one time, but he also said that wherever two or three are gathered together in his name, he is in the midst of them. Numbers cannot therefore reflect spiritual values, but statistics are nevertheless very important to discern trends and to determine if you are achieving your goals. There's also nothing wrong in doing everything within your power to increase attendance, in order that more may hear the message.

One Lenten season, when we were trying to beef up our poorly attended Sunday evening services, we found that competition can sometimes be used as a means of enlarging the circle of hearers of the Word. We asked each organization of the congregation to sponsor one of the Sunday evenings, taking upon itself the responsibility for ushering, assisting in the worship leadership, and sparking the attendance. Even before the series of services started, it was evident that a genuine rivalry had developed among them to see which would have the best representation. Since membership numbers were unequal, we determined that the organization which had the highest percentage of its membership present would be the "winner."

Attendance picked up remarkably on those Sunday evenings. To everyone's surprise, the Men's Club turned out the best percentage of members—and on a Sunday evening! But all the groups showed genuine enthusiasm for participating in the game. Competition adds spice!

A numerical goal can also help you in the church school. In our case, we had flirted with a Sunday morning attendance of five hundred for several months. We got close to it, but we needed some extra stimulus if we were to reach that figure before the summer slump cut down attendance. After Easter, we made our appeal to the school's pupils, asking them not to let attendance decline, but to try to have every child present on the first Sunday in May. We hoped that the warm and sunny Sundays of May would be "500 days." The bad weather and the wintertime sniffles that kept some children home would not then be a factor.

Youngsters always like to do things that sound like games, and they supported the effort willingly. Sure enough, on the first Sunday in May we topped five hundred. Better yet, we stayed above five hundred for three of the four Sundays in May. Once the goal had been attained, it was easier to remain at that level.

When full activity resumed the following fall, there was great interest among the school's leaders and pupils in the attendance marks posted each Sunday. This was a residual benefit from the achievement in May, and we capitalized on it. A small banner was given to each class that had 100 percent attendance, and most tried to be "banner classes." Each of the youngsters seemed to take personal pride in the effort. Whether or not this contributed to their spiritual growth, it obviously contributed to their enthusiasm for their church and to their willingness to work toward higher goals. There's value in that, too.

Church attendance is likewise a valuable barometer of the enthusiasm of the congregation. Attendance should be recorded carefully, Sunday after Sunday. When averages have been established over several years, it becomes possible to see at a glance if attendance is growing, holding steady, or declining. When the latter occurs, you get ample early warning of danger ahead. Why are fewer people

Using large index cards, make a file with a separate card for each member family. In that way you'll have a great amount of information at your finger tips—wedding anniversaries, birthdays, hobbies, special interests, and membership records.

Name _____ Telephone _____

Address _____

Husband's name _____ Wife's name _____

Born _____ at _____ Born _____ at _____

Baptized _____ Confirmed _____ Baptized _____ Confirmed _____

Former church _____ Former church _____

Interests _____ Interests _____

Business _____ Business _____ Married _____

CHILDREN:	Birth	Bapt.	Conf.	College
_____	_____	_____	_____	_____
_____	_____	_____	_____	_____
_____	_____	_____	_____	_____
_____	_____	_____	_____	_____
_____	_____	_____	_____	_____
_____	_____	_____	_____	_____
_____	_____	_____	_____	_____
_____	_____	_____	_____	_____
_____	_____	_____	_____	_____

coming to worship? Is it lagging enthusiasm, poor preaching, inadequate music, or a sign of a declining neighborhood?

Maintaining a simple graph showing church attendance sometimes does wonders to stimulate people. This graph shows the peaks and valleys of the year. Almost everywhere there's a period of decline due to summer vacations, winter storms, or something else. But in the course of two or three years, by superimposing the attendance graph of one year over that of another, you can readily see what's happening to your congregation. Just as a fever chart at a patient's bedside can help a physician, an attendance chart can help a pastor diagnose the condition of the congregation.

Accurate record-keeping is also important for congregations. To know at any given time how many members are on the rolls, how many are active, how many faithfully attend services, and how many commune is an essential part of the church's history. Some denominations require such figures for the annual report of the congregation. Even if there is no such denominational pressure, we should not be slothful in the business of record-keeping. It's a measure of the health of the congregation and also a good indicator for future planning.

Pastors with large congregations have found that a large index card bearing all pertinent information about members can be helpful. Although it takes time to keep entries on the card current, each card might list each family by name, address, special interests, organizational membership, names and birthdates of children, and other pertinent information.

12.

Encourage Your Artists!

During the Middle Ages, the arts were devoted almost exclusively to the service of the church. Great painting was chiefly of a religious nature. Music was centered in the worship services. Even literature dealt largely with theological themes and doctrinal matters. Maybe the last few centuries have seen too great a separation between religion and the arts. The church has become bereft since the arts are now secularized.

Your congregation can help restore the church to its rightful position as a patron of the arts by opening its doors to artists and musicians. Your church is a natural setting for art exhibits, musical programs, and other cultural events. To make your church a cultural center will take time and planning, as everything worthwhile does, but it will enhance the stature of your congregation among an important segment of your community, and your members will respond eagerly to the chance to increase their acquaintance with and taste for the fine arts.

Music is the art form most closely related to churches. Almost every church has an organ, encourages congregational singing, and may even have a musical organization like a choir. Unfortunately church music sometimes seems to suffer by comparison with secular music. Young people are exposed to good music in school and college. Radio, television, and records bring the talents of the greatest musicians into the homes of your people. It takes effort and initiative to maintain the church's musical program at an acceptable level of excellence.

Maybe you're overlooking some available talent.

Why not augment your church music and dip into this pool of talent by staging a music festival? Such a festival can utilize the talents of the organist and choir, but it should include others. You may have young people who play in a school band or orchestra. Why not bring their talents into the church? Or in your community there are sure to be persons who have had voice lessons and who are good singers, and persons who are proficient in playing some instrument. To develop their talents and their stage presence, such performers need an audience. They'll be glad to participate as part of your music festival.

In New York, where a wealth of talent is available, one congregation with an excellent choir and musical staff presents a Bach cantata every Sunday afternoon from October to May. Music lovers crowd the church in such numbers that there's standing room only, and sometimes an overflow out in the street. A short worship service and sermon are part of the program, thus enabling the church to extend its mission into the lives of hundreds of people who would otherwise be untouched by it.

A few blocks away in the same city, another church is noted for its "Jazz Vespers" held every Sunday evening with well-known professional jazz musicians donating their talents as an act of worship. Here too the church is able to reach out to an otherwise neglected segment of the community.

In a small southern city, a congregation found that an excellent instrumental music program in the public schools was equipping many of its teenagers to perform well on a variety of instruments. These young musicians were persuaded to bring their talents into the church, assisting as soloists for preludes or offertories, or simply strengthening the instrumental leadership of hymns. There's something stirring about a rousing hymn led by a strong organ and a quartet of trumpets! Such participation added greatly to the effectiveness of this church's musical program and also offered an outlet for the talents of some budding musicians.

And what about the visual arts? Every community has many "Sunday painters." They're eager to show off their productions, even if they're amateurish or primitive. Clothesline art exhibitions held in parks or commercial malls draw exhibitors from miles around. Beside painting, drawing, and etching, there are exhibits of handmade jewelry, sculpture, and other crafts. Artists are always proud of their creations and crave any chance to show off their talents to the public. Why doesn't your church help them and itself by providing the setting for an exhibit?

One suburban congregation found that among its members were many devotees of art who were willing to plan and conduct an exhibit at the church. To assure that professional artists would exhibit, the group raised funds to provide prizes for the best works in the show. It also arranged for several prominent local artists and art critics to act as a jury to select the best pieces. More than three hundred works of art were delivered to the church and placed either on the walls or on specially built panels. With such great participation, persons interested in art, and others who were simply curious, came in great numbers to attend the exhibition. The festival was so successful that it has become an annual event which attracts attention throughout art circles in the entire metropolitan area. The congregation now has a reputation as a great patron of the arts! So can yours!

Invitations to exhibit should first go to artists in your congregation. They'll form the nucleus for your sponsoring committee. It may be the best chance for their works to rub elbows, so to speak, with those of topnotch artists. Local art clubs, art classes in public schools or nearby colleges, and art supply dealers should be notified and asked to post announcements of the exhibit.

If artists are permitted to put a price tag on their works and offer them for sale, some will probably be purchased and the church can claim a small percentage (usually 10 percent) of the purchase price. This could pay all the costs for the exhibition, in some cases. However, whether or not the art exhibit breaks even isn't important. The chief benefit isn't in cash, but in the reputation your congregation will get for encouraging art and artists.

Incidentally, thieves may break in and steal, even in church. If valuable art works are left overnight, round-the-clock protection should be provided. It's also possible to obtain low-cost insurance to cover any loss while the art is in your care.

Another cultural adventure that has worked well for many churches is a lecture series or an adult education program. If your community lacks this cultural advantage, you can lead the way and develop a simple program that will be meaningful both to your members and to the community. Educational services reach into the lives of people of all faiths and expand the influence of your congregation.

Let's say that you feel there's a need in your community for information in the field of family relations—how to be a better husband, wife, parent, lover. You know that many of your members, young and old, would benefit from information and open discussion of these topics. The first step after ascertaining the need is to consult with congregational leaders, to be assured of their support for the program and their assistance in sponsoring it. If your congregation is strong enough to support such a series alone, fine. But if it isn't, contact other community leaders—school teachers and administrators, physicians, public officials, other ministers. Invite their advice and support. Maybe they'll help you find a lecturer who can lead the courses. It could be a college professor who teaches social science, a lawyer who specializes in marital counseling. Make sure that the viewpoints likely to be expressed by the lecturer are in accord with those of your church! And plan well in advance, because a good lecturer is likely to be booked far ahead.

Your lecturer may have a set fee for a series of lectures or may be willing to accept an amount proportionate to the number who enroll in the course. The latter is a better deal for you. Let's say the fee is $500 for five lectures. You would then have to sign up 100 people, each willing to pay $5 for the course. That would be a bargain rate today, for in almost any community that's far less than people pay for the movies. But here again, whether or not the program pays for itself is less important than the fact that you are contributing an essential educational service and encouraging the intellectual and cultural development of the people.

13.

Who's at Church?

In a large congregation, it's impossible for the pastor to identify each person in the pews. A few pastors gifted with photographic memories claim to remember each person they greet at the church door, but such claims are hard to verify. Wouldn't it help you to know, week after week, who is at church?

A Florida congregation uses weekly attendance-taking to excellent advantage. The attendance list provides a source of names of prospective members and also a means of determining who's absent so that proper concern can be shown.

During an interlude in the service called the "Fellowship of Friendship" period, ushers distribute specially made forms to the person at the end of each pew. The ruled sheets are marked so that each worshiper can write down his name, address, and, if the person is a visitor, the name of his or her home church. The sheets are clipped to a hard board to make writing easier. The pastor of this congregation notes that by signing this list and passing it along, worshipers learn the names of those sitting near them and are able to greet one another by name. "People from the same northern community have met for the first time in our pews," the pastor says.

It takes only a minute or two for this sheet to be passed along the pew. It is then collected at the other side. Very few people are unwilling to place their names on the sheet.

Since this congregation has an average of a thousand persons at its Saturday evening and Sunday services, coordinating the lists is a good-sized job. However, volunteers come into the church office each Monday morning and get it done in a few hours. They type the names of visitors and nonmembers on a special list. If the residence of these persons is far away, they are sent a note of welcome and an invitation to come back when they're again in that section of Florida. If they list an address somewhere within the parish bounds or indicate a special interest in the congregation, they get a visit within the week from one of the congregation's "ministers of evangelism."

The names of members attending the services are divided into nine geographical zones into which the congregation is divided. The responsible zone leader then reviews the list and checks off those from his area who attended the services. When a member has failed to attend for several Sundays, a follow-up is made either by telephone or by a personal visit. Often this can uncover cases of illness or special need. The pastoral staff is then apprised of the situation promptly so that proper care can be provided.

If your congregation is small, an individual's absence is easy to note. But when it includes hundreds of people, some system like this is needed to keep you in touch with each of your members.

This attendance registration form was developed by St. Mark Church, Dunedin, Florida, and is used there at every service. The form is clipped to a piece of hard board, to make writing easier, and is passed along the pew.

ATTENDANCE REGISTRATION FOR ALL PRESENT							DATE_____
NAME	ADDRESS, TELEPHONE, ZIP CODE	MEMBER OF THIS CHURCH	WISH TO JOIN THIS CHURCH	DESIRE A CALL	NEW RESIDENT	VISITOR IN THE CITY	IF A VISITOR, PLEASE LIST YOUR CHURCH AND ADDRESS

Section II
Increasing Outreach

14.

Get Your Picture on Page One

In American newspapers, you can't buy a big display advertisement on the front page. For one thing, the cost would be prohibitive. But you can get your picture on Page One any time you choose to. It all depends on the timing. Whether you're in a major metropolis, a medium-sized city, or a small town, the technique is the same. By following the method outlined below, it's just not possible to miss, no matter what area you're in and no matter how uninterested the local press seems to be in church affairs.

Here's how to do it:

Most churches try to do something special for festival occasions, whether it is in the altar decorations, special displays, pageantry, or music. The secret for getting maximum publicity for whatever you're doing is to come up with something photogenic that's representative of the particular season.

For Thanksgiving, this could be a harvest display built around a specially designed cross (see sample on next page). The cross can also be used as the theme for Good Friday. For Christmas, the photo might be of some pageantry involving children. For another occasion, it can be a display especially adapted to some other theme.

For example, in a "Christ for the world" observance, we used two round disks, actually two disk sleds about thirty inches in diameter. We then pasted maps on the two sleds, showing on one, North and South America and on the other, Asia, Africa, and Europe. Then we took carpenter's glue and covered just the land masses with it. To the glue (before it dried) we affixed kernels of yellow corn, one at a time. These were dry kernels like the kind used for popcorn. Then we painted another batch of corn kernels blue and similarly affixed them to the ocean areas. The result was a striking map, the continents covered in golden corn contrasting with the blue oceans.

When the reporter came to photograph the two globes, he asked how many kernels of corn we had used. Actually we had no idea, but he said to take a guess, so we told him 431,000. "That's amazing!" he said. That figure was printed in the paper, and everyone was very much impressed by it.

As mentioned above, timing is important. If you pay attention to your timing, when you have this kind of display you can't miss getting on the front page.

In the case of our Thanksgiving display, we had one month earlier contacted the editor of the local paper, offering to assist him with a striking Thanksgiving theme for his Thanksgiving Day issue. We explained that we were planning to set up the cross on the weekend before Thanksgiving and would complete the chancel decorations on Monday, so that by Tuesday morning the display would be complete and ready to photograph. This schedule was followed exactly, and on Tuesday the newspaper's photographer came, took the picture, and we were on the front page on Thanksgiving Day!

For a picture that will appear on the front page on the Thursday when Thanksgiving is celebrated, the display must be prepared at least five days in advance. The newspaper must also be given adequate advance notice.

In our case, we built the cross on the Saturday before Thanksgiving. It took about three hours to go to the lumber yard, buy the lumber, nail the boards together, drive the four hundred nails through the boards, and set the fruit between the nails. A blueprint for building such a cross is sampled.

Sunday afternoon we set up the cross in the church auditorium so that on Monday night the members of the church could come in to help complete the decorations. For the cross, we bought a case of red apples and a case of yellow apples. Members brought in some pumpkins and other harvest decorations like colored leaves and wheat sheaves. The total cost was small.

In order not to damage the fruit, the apples were set between the nails that protruded through the cross, alternating the red and yellow varieties. A spray of wheat was placed at the center of the cross and the pumpkins were stacked around the base. The whole process was simple and inexpensive, yet the result was very impressive.

By following our schedule strictly, the product of our efforts was ready for photographing early on Tuesday, thereby assuring the editor that he would have his Thanksgiving theme picture in ample time. Editors get nervous when deadlines are not met.

Similar advance planning is needed for other occasions when you want to make the front page. Newspapers are always a little anxious about Good Friday. They know it's a major religious holiday, but one which does not lend itself to exploitation like Christmas, or even Easter. By following a schedule similar to that for a Thanksgiving picture, you can assure that a photograph of a black-draped cross in your church auditorium will get top attention from the local press.

If you will take the trouble to set up your display sufficiently in advance of the holiday and offer it to the local paper as a timely treatment of the event, which they can photograph and process at their convenience in ample time for their editions, you are going to get a great spot in the paper. There's no money in the world that can buy this kind of highly favorable publicity treatment for your church, but you can have it free if you work it right.

By following these detailed plans, making the special "Thanks-giving Cross" is easy. The photo shows the completed project in the setting that got it big space in the local newspaper.

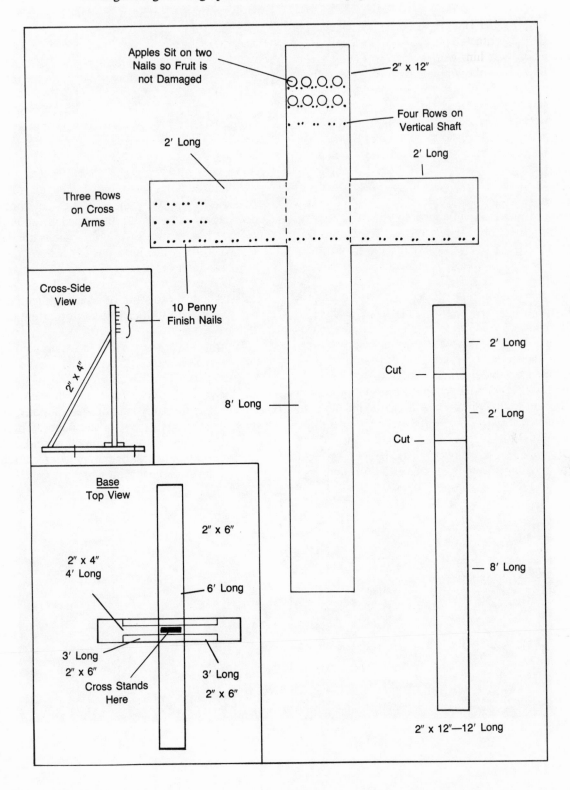

Apples Sit on two Nails so Fruit is not Damaged

2" x 12"

Four Rows on Vertical Shaft

2' Long

2' Long

Three Rows on Cross Arms

Cross-Side View

10 Penny Finish Nails

2" x 4"

8' Long

2' Long

Cut

2' Long

Cut

8' Long

Base Top View

2" x 6"

2" x 4" 4' Long

6' Long

3' Long 2" x 6"

3' Long 2" x 6"

Cross Stands Here

2" x 12"—12' Long

15.

It Pays to Advertise

For thirty years or more the Committee on Religion in American Life (RIAL) has done an excellent job of keeping the American public aware of the importance of religion in the life of the nation. Using newspapers, magazines, radio, and television, the committee has worked with the Advertising Council to get its message across. Air time for the RIAL campaign is donated by the stations and space in the periodicals is donated by the publishers. The campaign itself is planned and developed by expert advertising people on a volunteer basis. In all, millions of dollars worth of free publicity are given annually to a worthy cause.

In a similar way, you need to use the finest facilities available to you to keep your community aware of the place of your church in its life. Advertising is important. The best advertising, of course, is by word of mouth as your parishioners "talk up" the church and live out their faith in their daily lives. The pastor is also able to help the congregation by participating in public life, serving the community freely, and representing the church well. Your church building itself can be a good advertisement or a bad one (see chapter 20).

But beyond all this, you need to use the public press and all other media to establish a high recognition factor for your church. Aside from news, which is dealt with elsewhere, you will find that it pays to pay to advertise. Taking a paid advertisement in a small newspaper is a symbol of your support for that paper and is likely to influence their willingness to give you space for news. A paid advertisement in a large newspaper, which really doesn't need your ad, is both a prestige item for your church and a way of reaching a wide audience of readers.

To be effective, a newspaper advertisement must be clear and straightforward. It should not be cluttered with too many words or deal with too many different topics. Let the ad tell about your Sunday services; if you have a weekday program, take a special ad on a different day to announce it. Trying to put too much information into one church ad may lead readers to skip over it, since the competition for attention is keen.

On a typical Saturday "church page" a dozen or more churches may be represented by paid advertisements (see sample). Your ad should have some distinctive factor to make it stand out among the crowd. This might be the use of special type, but you need expert guidance if you go this route. It could also be the use of some striking slogan or an excerpt from your sermon, but here you risk trying to pour in too much and therefore losing the attention of the reader. Best is to have some special logo, photograph, or drawing that makes your ad distinctive and that can be repeated over and over, thereby increasing the recognition factor. People who are actually *looking* for information about your church will soon recognize your particular format. Since many newspapers use photo-offset production, a simple drawing like the one in the sample ad can easily be reproduced. If your paper still uses letterpress, they will make a "cut" of your drawing or photograph for a small cost. The metal cut can be used over again many times.

Don't think that you can advertise once a year and have people remember your church. One secret of successful commercial advertising is constant repetition. We see some commercials on television so often that we become tired of them, but whether we like them or dislike them, we remember them. Advertising for recognition takes hold when it's pounded home time after time. And even the fiftieth time an ad appears may be the first time some newcomer spots it!

Printed or handmade posters are a form of advertising often neglected by churches. Merchants and commercial establishments are usually willing to place such posters in a prominent place. When there's a special service or other special event at your church, you can use a poster announcement with good results. Posters must be eye-catching and colorful. Members of your congregation with some artistic ability can be enlisted to produce this "poster ministry." They're likely to have new and innovative ideas for the use of such posters. One word of warning: be a good neighbor and DO NOT tack posters up on trees or poles where they are unsightly and unwanted. A second word of warning: after the event, remove the posters. Nothing looks more careless than a poster announcing an event that took place two weeks ago.

16.

Enlist Ma Bell

Many churches do not take full advantage of modern communications. For example, your local telephone company has dozens of varieties of different services it can offer. Too often we think of the telephone as a thing to be used only for personal calls. Yet there are dial-a-prayers, dial-a-jokes, and dial-almost-everything. Many different possibilities ought to be explored by any church to get the most value from its telephone—for instance, an inexpensive service to keep your church in business twenty-four hours a day. It takes only a simple answering device.

In our weekly church ad we always listed a telephone number with the request that for further information about services readers call that number. When people called (and quite a few did), they heard a recorded message that invited them to attend church, gave them the hours of services and the pastor's sermon topic, along with announcements of special music or special speakers. Anything unusual planned for the week was also mentioned in the brief announcement, along with an invitation to callers to stay for the coffee hour after services in order to get acquainted.

The telephone company can suggest a multitude of similar services that can be used by anyone. It would pay any church to call up the local telephone company, or its special representative, to discuss the way the telephone can be made most useful in its program. Every telephone office has experts to advise you on these specialties. They may also try to sell you a special phone system which you may or may not need, but you don't have to take anything you don't want. Choose only the special services that seem best to fit your needs.

Telephone rates are controlled, so services the phone company can offer are usually quite reasonable, especially in view of the depth and dimension they'll add to the work of your church. Some of their suggestions may be extremely innovative. At least, they're worth a try. So call in the telephone representatives and talk to them. If they can't help you immediately, at least you'll get to know them and what their company can offer. On their side, once they find out you are eager to increase the use of the telephone in your ministry, they'll make every effort to help. When new devices, ranging from answering services to mobile telephones in your car, to recorded

One of these church ads stands out from the others—and not only because the author's name appears on it.

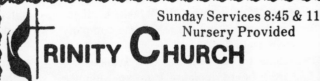

Sunday Services 8:45 & 11
Nursery Provided
RINITY CHURCH

United Methodist
9625 N. Military Tr.•Palm Beach Gardens

COMMUNITY CHURCH
Park Ave. at 5th St.   Lake Park

**INVITES YOU TO WORSHIP WITH US
EACH SUNDAY**

Jr. Hi., Sr. Hi., Adult Sunday School	9 a.m.
Divine Worship	10 a.m.
Youth Sunday School	10 a.m.

Walter W. Wynkoop, D.D., Pastor
Mrs. Jane Mudgett, Music Director

**St. John's
Church**
Sunday School 9 a.m.
Worship Service 10 a.m.
241 Cypress Dr., Lake Park
(2 Blks. west of Hwy. One)
848-3142

"Your Church"
NORTH PALM BEACH, FLORIDA
WORSHIP SERVICES 8:00 & 10:45 A.M.
BIBLE STUDY (ALL AGES) 9:15 A.M.
(NURSERY at all Services)
PASTOR'S FORUM 9:30 A.M.
COFFEE FELLOWSHIP 9:00-9:30 A.M.

Sermon: **"Things That Cannot Be Shaken"**
**Guest Preacher
Dr. Albert P. Stauderman**
848-4737

555 U.S. HIGHWAY ONE
Just north of Twin City Mall
**WEEKDAY NURSERY
KINDERGARTEN PROGRAM**

messages, to conference networks, become available, they'll be in touch with you promptly.

There are also one-shot telephone gimmicks that may work for you. Once when I was wintering in the cold North, I got a phone call from a former parishioner who had moved to Florida. "We'd like you to give a short talk to our congregation next Monday," he told me. I envisioned a plane trip to sunny Florida! But he continued, "You can speak right from your office at home. We'll make arrangements for a clear wire, and the telephone company will provide an amplifier here."

The call came through on the dot. I made the speech and even heard applause from an audience 1,200 miles away. While this was my first such experience, it was probably not unusual. I've heard of ministers who while hospitalized have spoken to their Sunday morning congregations in similar fashion.

Tape recordings can provide other opportunities for an extended ministry. Once I had an address scheduled for a meeting in St. Louis, when an invitation came to me to visit the Holy Land as the guest of the Israeli government. A colleague suggested that I tape my address, in that way fulfilling my commitment to the St. Louis audience without missing the Holy Land trip. This was done, and he took the tape to the meeting in St. Louis, where it was played for the audience. But to add to the novelty, he had suggested several questions which I answered on the tape. These questions were then "planted" among members of the audience. So after the taped presentation, my colleague asked for questions from the audience. The conspirators then rose to ask their questions, and my voice answered from the tape. It was a rather sensational conclusion for the address.

Many congregations have set up a telephone network in order to reach members quickly with important news or announcements. A Florida church has done this very efficiently, even though it has a membership of almost two thousand. Their "grape-vine" system enables them to contact every member household within a few minutes—except, of course,

those not at home or not answering their phones.

The message to be delivered requires phone calls from the church office to seven zone captains, each of whom is responsible for a certain area of the community. These zone captains then make calls to five key telephone committee members in their zone. By the time this is done, forty-two households have already been reached. Each committee member then has five calls to make, in each case asking the person called to convey the message to one or two of his neighbors. The thirty-five committee members reach 175 families. If each such family calls or reaches two others, a total of 562 households has been contacted. If the calls are kept short and to the point, it can probably all be done in ten minutes!

To make this system work, it must be carefully planned and used only in important matters or emergencies. But it works. When the pastor was hospitalized with a mild heart attack, within minutes the system assured him that hundreds of members of the congregation were united in prayer for his recovery. In a time of national emergency or in a congregational crisis, such a system could be an enormous blessing.

Using the telephone to aid the church's ministry is so obviously beneficial that one wonders why more churches don't do it. For instance, a phone call may be the simplest and most effective way to check up on members who haven't been seen at church for a while. Evangelism committees can make this one of their jobs. Where churches have registration for Communion or for church attendance, the telephone provides a quick and handy means of following up those who are absent. In almost every case they'll be grateful for the interest shown; and if they object to being followed up in this manner, it may indicate some more deep-seated problem for the pastor or other church leaders to look into.

One word of warning: don't use the telephone for soliciting funds! This has been done to death by secular organizations and is very often counter-productive.

17.

God Sent Me!

Part of our failure in evangelism may be due to confusion. We say we are doing evangelism when really we are simply recruiting members for our particular organization. Here's the definition of evangelism, taken from a popular dictionary: **Evangelism 1:** *a preaching of the Gospel; earnest effort for the spread of the Gospel* **2:** *the work of an evangelist* **3:** *belief in the doctrines of an evangelical church or party; evangelicalism.*

Now look at what it means to recruit: **Recruit 1:** *to fill up the number of (an army) with new members* **2:** *to increase or maintain the number of* **3:** *to enlist new members.*

Both evangelism and recruiting are important, but they're not the same. Which are you doing? Let Jim Morentz describe his experience:

When I first became a fulltime church worker, my job was to lead the laypersons of the congregation in the work laypersons ought to be doing—stewardship, evangelism, and promotion. Let me tell you I was an absolute sensation in stewardship and promotion, but fell flat on my face in evangelism. After three years I went to my second job, this time at First Lutheran Church in Los Angeles, but with one specific restriction—no evangelism!

Then it turned out that after a year or so we had a loss of membership, and they asked me if I would not take over the responsibility for evangelism and give it a try. So I got involved in following up the visitors to our services. We usually had about fifty visitors in the church on Sunday morning. Half of these were out-of-towners visiting in California, but the other half were people who lived somewhere in the vicinity and were therefore possible candidates for membership. Every Sunday we had members registration

cards which everyone attending filled out, including the guests. It was a helpful way of keeping in touch with our members, too, because the record showed when members were absent for a period of time and when a visit or call was needed to find out why and what we could do about it. It was a lot of work to keep these records, but a volunteer came into the church office every Monday morning and kept them up to date. Attendance cards from visitors were then turned over to me.

Out-of-town visitors were sent a picture postcard of the church with a note thanking them for worshiping with us. Local visitors were supposed to get a visit from me prior to the next Sunday. It meant five or more calls each evening. The first week I started with twenty-two cards and came up with only two people who were moderately interested. The second week there were twenty-four cards, but again I found only two people who showed any interest.

After a few weeks of this sort of thing, I sat down to decide why I was such a failure. And then it came to me: I was not doing evangelism, which was what the job called for; I was going out as a recruiter trying to sign somebody up for church membership. I had no intention of saving souls or changing peoples' lives or even of doing anything good for the world. I was just trying to add members to my church. On the other hand, most of the people I visited were drifters who attended various churches but didn't want the responsibility of membership in any of them.

Evangelism in its true form, I realized, seeks a commitment to Christ and his church. This commitment normally takes the form of membership in a specific congregation. Through this commitment to a congregation, a person works out his own needs and fits his talents into the whole, growing as a Christian

Your Invitation to
The Pastor's Class

"Your Church"

3119 West 6th Street
Los Angeles, Calif.

About the Pastor's Class

What Is the Pastor's Class?

A series of talks on the Christian religion, with full opportunity for questions and discussion—giving you opportunity to learn something of this Church **before** you become a member.

What Does It Cover?

The basic teachings of the Christian faith, the life and worship of the Lutheran Church, the benefits and responsibilities of membership.

Who Teaches It?

Pastor Click—with qualified laymen assisting during sessions on this congregation and its work.

Who May Attend?

Anyone is welcome. Members, too, are invited and often attend. But the content is planned to meet the specific needs of the inquiring non-member.

What Happens at the Conclusion?

You decide—not blindly, but with enlightenment—whether you will become a member of the First English Lutheran Church.

When Is It Held?

The next Pastor's Class series at First English Lutheran Church will begin Mar. 11 at 10:00 a.m. Child care will be provided.

Dear Pastor Click:

I accept the invitation of FIRST ENGLISH LUTHERAN CHURCH to attend the Pastor's Class with church membership in view, beginning March 11, at 10:00 a.m. Attendance does not obligate me to membership.

Name...

Address..

Zone.......... ....Telephone.....................

Schedule of the Pastor's Class:

March 11, 18, 25, — April 1, 8.
Reception of members on April 15 at the 11:00 a.m. Service.

If you are now ready to make a decision about membership, check below:

☐ I desire to become a member of First English Lutheran Church on April 15.

☐ I am a Lutheran and will unite by letter of transfer on April 15.

person and strengthening the Christian community.

So one Monday morning I decided on a new approach. I listed every church in our district of the city, no matter how weird it was—Scientology, anything. Then I called each church, telling them that we might have some prospects for membership. Usually when you hint to a minister that you may have a new member for him, he'll walk a mile for it! So they gladly furnished me with information about their church and the minister's home phone number. In all, I had thirty-one churches on my list.

Armed with this new approach, I went out and knocked on the door of my first prospects. When they opened the door, I said "Hi, the Lord sent me. I came to see that you join a church tonight."

They looked me over. There are all kinds of odd religions in California, but I looked fairly normal and presentable. So they said, "What?"

"God sent me," I repeated. "I came to see that you join a church tonight."

Then just before they slammed the door, I added, "Didn't you attend the First Lutheran Church last Sunday?" Of course, they said that they had, and then I told them that I was from First Lutheran Church and they let me in. At least in most cases they let me in.

"How long have you been in Los Angeles?" I would ask. They'd tell me six months or eight months. "In all that time you've been visiting churches, and whenever someone asked you to join a church you ducked? Well, this is your night not to duck! The Lord sent me here, and you're going to join a church tonight. By the way, how did you like the service?"

They'd say it was fine, and I'd ask if they wanted to become a member. Then they'd say, "Well, we also attended the Baptist Church."

So I'd say, "Oh, that's a splendid church. Would you like to join the Baptist Church?" They'd say, "Oh, we visit around. We went to the Episcopal Church and the Presbyterian Church, too." At this point I took my list of churches out of my pocket and said, "You're in luck. On this paper I have the names of all the churches and ministers in the area. I'll call

any one of these pastors, and I'm sure he'll be over here before the evening is over because you are a believer in the gospel, and the best way to live out the gospel is as a member of a church, so I want you to join a church tonight."

I knew that these people had attended various churches occasionally, but I also knew that I had a psychological advantage. They couldn't remember what the other churches were like, but they'd been at my church just a few days before. Naturally they'd remember it best.

As we conversed, I could feel that they were leaning more and more to making a commitment, but I kept saying, "I don't care where you join, but you must make up your mind."

Inevitably, the husband or the wife would break. One would say, "You know, we've been attending different churches ever since we moved down here, and we ought to make up our minds. I think this man came here with a mission and this is the day."

From that point on, I would go out early in the week with twenty or more cards from visitors, and if I didn't come back with most of them signed up for the pastor's class it was a bad week. But it happened only because I asked them for positive action in response to their belief. That's the difference between evangelism and recruitment.

To follow up on this, some people said to me, "You're a salesman. You can go out with this kind of approach, but I can't." That's not true. I chose various other lay people to come out with me on these visits, asking them to do nothing but accompany me and watch. I told them, "You are watching what I do and what the response is. Keep thinking of yourself, how can I do what he does and make happen what is happening?" Naturally, each person had to develop his own approach, one that he was comfortable with. But by the end of a year, some of these people developed the ability to speak out persuasively. Soon my job was a lot easier because we had a trained and devoted group that could go out in an "earnest effort to spread the gospel." And that's evangelism.

18.
Feed the Press

Remember the biblical story about the man who used the talents his master loaned to him and got good interest on them? That was a form of investment that paid off handsomely, and in addition the lord praised him for being a good steward. A similar investment that can pay off for you is a luncheon and advice session for representatives of the press, radio, and television outlets in your area.

Invite the religion editor from the local paper or the correspondent who writes the items about your territory for the newspaper that serves your area. Also invite columnists, commentators, talk show hosts, disc jockeys, or newscasters from local radio and television stations. Take them to a nice restaurant for lunch. You'll spend two or three bucks, but it will be the best investment you can make if you follow the simple suggestions below.

At the luncheon, do not try to give them a sales talk about your church program. They'll come suspiciously, with the idea that you have something you want mentioned in the paper or on the air. Your approach must be different. Ask them three questions, and then let them do the talking! The questions:

How do we best get mention in your medium?

What do you consider to be news?

What do we have that might be considered news from our church?

In your preparation for the luncheon, make up a list of events that will take place at your church during the next few months. Have the list typed up in simple and attractive form. It will include routine services and educational sessions, of course. But there may also be events recognizing church workers, installation of new equipment, "graduations" from kindergarten into first grade, and other such items. Hand the list to your assembled experts (have a copy for each one so none will feel slighted) and ask them, "Would these things be news? It not, how could we make them become news that's worth printing or announcing on the air?"

Sometimes a little twist in the way you present a program may turn something into news. News isn't always important or earth-shaking. If it's interesting and attention-grabbing, it has a good chance of getting into print or on the air.

Don't feel hesitant about inviting the press to your luncheon. Religion writers are often the newest and lowest paid persons on a newspaper staff. Local correspondents or "stringers" for a county newspaper are often paid by the column inch, so the more information they can channel to a paper the better off they will be. They'll enjoy the lunch, and you'll get a lot of free advice about how to get your church into the news.

After the luncheon, don't hesitate to keep in touch with them. Call them from time to time to ask, "Is this a story?" If you'll do this consistently, the coverage given your church will definitely increase, maybe many times over.

Don't skimp on the luncheon! It will cost some money, but there's always somebody in your church who has money to contribute and who says, "How come we never see anything about our church in the paper?" You can tell this person, "I have a great idea to get publicity for our church and its program, but it will cost about $50. How about picking up the tab? I'll gladly arrange the meeting with the press, radio, and television people, and it will be a good investment on your part for the future of our church."

Remember: this is an advice session, not a news conference. It aims to provide you with contacts and information that can continually be helpful. A news conference is a one-shot deal, and unless your news is really important it may leave the press less than enthused. But by asking their advice and help, you flatter them and build up their ego and eventually make their job easier. You make an investment that will continue to bear dividends for a long time to come.

19.
Man or Woman of the Year

As a publicity stunt that also has some validity as a recognition of Christian service, select a "Man of the Year" or "Woman of the Year." The event that surrounds the presentation of an award or a plaque to this person is a sure-fire attention-getter for the press, radio, and television.

In our church at Pittsburgh, we developed the "Man of the Year" event to stimulate our noon-day services, which were attended largely by people from the downtown business community. It was essential, of course, for our choice to be supportable from the standpoint of both character and church relationship. The first such award was given to Roy W. Johnson, then head of NASA. The award plaque read, "To Roy W. Johnson for making an outstanding contribution in relating Christian principles to daily vocation." Each year thereafter we tried to recognize a national leader who really did live out his Christian ideals in his daily work.

In our case, we invited the award recipient to be at one of the services, where the presentation would be made. Usually this involved meeting the person at the airport, and here we were fortunate because a prominent local industry loaned us a limousine and a chauffeur to bring our award-winner into the city. Following the service, we invited business executives to a high-level reception held at the church. Here again we were lucky, for another industry picked up the tab for the cost of the reception! Obviously, that can't happen everywhere. But we had written to the major industrial companies in the area asking them to list no more than ten of their top executives whom they would like us to invite to the reception. The response was excellent. It brought us favorable attention from these companies and provided us with a list of local business leaders whom we could call upon year after year for support of the noon-day services. We knew that each of these persons had attended a service and reception in our church and was aware of the program we were trying to conduct. No matter what their religious faith was, we knew that each of them was therefore likely to be supportive of the program.

The Pittsburgh program was a large-scale effort and cannot be followed in detail by most congregations. However, in every community there are opportunities for similar attention-getters. In a small town, the award might go to the mayor of the town, if he is a faithful churchman, or to the owner of some local industry, the publisher of the newspaper, or the operator of the television station. It could be a school principal or a doctor or a lawyer. The award should go to some person who stands out from the crowd by relating Christian principles to daily vocation. There are many such persons!

Whether the award is a large-scale affair or a very modest one, make your choice carefully. Set up a special devotional event to surround the presentation. Follow it with a reception in honor of the recipient of the award. Get a good list of prominent friends and associates of the person you are honoring and invite them to attend. And through it all, keep your publicity committee working hard! You have a major community event in your congregation, and it deserves recognition from the media!

There's another facet to this kind of award, however. In your own congregation you have people who deserve special mention—faithful teachers, devoted choir members, and leaders of organizations. Don't hestitate to honor them publicly! Too often we ignore the faithful everyday work done by loyal church members, who will never make the headlines of the newspaper, but who are important to the congregation. Along with your big media event in making a public award to a prominent local figure, pay some attention to the workers who keep your congregational program going by quiet service that doesn't make waves.

20.
Your Church Building Talks!

Does your church have a "Do Not Enter" sign in front of it? Here's what puts a "Do Not Enter" sign in front of your church: the grass isn't cut, the shrubs are overgrown, the building needs painting, the front walk is cracked, a window pane is broken, nobody has swept the walk, some letters are missing on your sign. When this is the case, your church is saying to everyone who passes by, "Nobody cares!" And when you have a church that says nobody cares, you might as well put up a big "Do Not Enter" sign out in front.

But suppose the outside is perfect. The visitor walks past well-groomed lawns and shrubs and up neatly swept steps and into the narthex, foyer, lobby, or whatever you call your entrance hall. What's there? Is it clean and orderly, with friendly greeters or ushers? Or is there a table messed up with old pamphlets, bulletins, and papers? Does it smell musty, as if the church were closed up 99 percent of the time?

And then the visitor finally gets to the pew. Does the visitor get the feeling that the seat ought to be dusted off before it can be occupied? And then what does the visitor do? Sit there feeling like an intruder? Or like a welcome guest?

The attitude of your ushers can make a big difference in whether or not people come back for a second time—a pleasant greeting, not too effusive, and some indication of help with the service! If you have a printed order of service in the bulletin or elsewhere, make sure that your visitor knows about it. It's greatly helpful if the usher or some regular worshiper will open the hymnal or service book to the right page and hand it to the visitor. Maybe the order of service begins on page 57, and it might take the visitor the whole hour of worship to find the right place.

The printed bulletin tells a tale, too. If it's a third-rate mimeograph job or a confused jumble of announcements and lists of hymns, it doesn't help the visitor, and instead says to him, "You're on your own, bud, in this church!"

The atmosphere has a message, too. If people visit back and forth before the service, talking in stage whispers and socializing, the visitor may feel like a fish out of water. Everybody is having a good time except him. They're saying, "Don't come back."

When the minister enters, his demeanor as well as his dress says a great deal. As he walks up the aisle, if his pants are too short, his robe's on crooked, his shoes aren't shined, and his hair rumpled and unkempt, he's part of that sign that says "Do Not Enter"!

It can't be emphasized too much that your building broadcasts a message. It should say, "This congregation is proud of its church. It's God's house and we keep it that way, not like some neglected shack."

It's the job of everybody in the congregation to help maintain the church's property. If they don't have the money to engage competent caretakers and repair people, they ought to have the time to devote to doing the work themselves. Nobody is too poor to give a few hours to a clean-up, fix-up, paint-up program. Just cutting the lawn and trimming the shrubs regularly can be somebody's major contribution to the congregation. It helps create a neat look that says to the world, "This is our church, and we care about it."

Even if your building is newly painted and glistening white, the lawns carefully manicured and the walkways swept, it may still say "Do Not Enter." Is there a sign telling the hours of services? And if the congregation generally uses a side entrance or a back door, does the visitor know about this? How many times have visitors wrestled with the locked front door of a church only to learn, finally, that for some reason a side door is used as the main entrance. A simple, small sign can convey this information. Without it, you may be telling visitors, "Do Not Enter!"

Most difficult is to find the church office or pastor's study. People who have some reason to come to the church during the week may have to circle the whole building, trying every door, before they find out where the pastor or secretary can be found. Everything says to the visitor, "You're not welcome here. Regular members know their way around, we'll let you be embarrassed"!

Stand out in front of your church and listen. Is it saying "Welcome," or is it saying "Do Not Enter"?

21.
Getting on the Air

About a thousand television stations and some sixty-two hundred radio stations (AM and FM) are licensed to operate in the United States. Those figures compare with 1,759 daily newspapers. It's clear that radio and television have become major media for the dissemination of news and information as well as for entertainment. Getting your church mentioned on radio or TV can be a big plus for your program. How do you go about it?

Remember, first of all, that most radio and TV stations are commercial operations. If you want

straight out advertising for your church, you had better plan to pay the station's rates. The same applies if you hope to broadcast your services or addresses. Even on the so-called religious radio stations, fees for broadcast time are needed so the stations can operate.

Broadcasters are under no obligation to provide free air time for anybody. Most stations, however, take pride in serving their communities by contributing public service time. This time is made available to nonprofit groups, and that includes churches and religious organizations of the community. There is no reason why you should not get your church on the air.

Your first step is to choose a station that seems to use the kind of material you will offer. If you think you'd like to be on an interview show, a 24-hour hard-rock station is not your likely host! But almost every station has some news programs and almost all air spot-announcements on a variety of topics, in addition to their paid commercials.

Every station has a program director, whose job is to plan well in advance what will be on the air. After you've selected the station you think should broadcast your message, call the program director and try to get a face-to-face appointment. If he or she just says, "Send me a sample of your stuff, and I'll look at it," you may be getting a brush-off. When you meet the program director, tell him or her what you're trying to get across to the listeners, who you expect will be the most interested segment of the audience, and how you plan to put the message across. This calls for a little homework and advance preparation on your part, but it's essential.

Remember also that commercial stations must carry free public service announcements only for non-profit organizations and events. If you're staging a raffle or trying to sell tickets, your announcement is commercial and must be paid for.

If the program director seems receptive, chances are that you'll be asked to provide either a spot-announcement, which the station will put on the air when there's a minute of free time, or to simply send in news which the station itself will attempt to work into its news broadcasts. Brief items are most likely to be handled successfully by a congregation or church organization. While you may have ideas for a 30-minute speech or a lengthy program by your church choir, remember that a lively and well-done 30-second announcement may be much more effective. Radio listeners tune out hurriedly when they're bored!

If you send in copy to be used by the station's own announcers on live broadcasts, follow the rules of good copy preparation. This includes clear typing, straightforward language, and the inclusion of all the necessary facts. The old newspaper adage for reporters holds good here: your announcement should tell who, what, where, when, how, and why.

If you are sending news copy, make sure it's sent in well in advance. It takes time for the station to work it into its programs, and "news" of what happened yesterday isn't useful!

Personal appearances on either radio or television are another matter and usually require expert assistance. If you are wealthy enough to buy time for this sort of thing, enlist the aid of a professional broadcaster or public relations agency. Nothing is worse than to fall flat on your face in front of thousands of TV watchers.

Can you get on the air? Even occasional listening to some of the local radio stations in various parts of the country indicates their willingness to cooperate with churches and religious organizations in providing free time for their announcements and news of their activities. You ought to claim your share!

Here are two announcements that made it:

Student recognition Sunday will be observed this week at First Lutheran Church, 2740 Parker Avenue, West Palm Beach. College students home for vacation will take part in both the 8:45 and 11 o'clock services, and a brass quartet from Palm Beach Junior College will provide special music. Dr. Albert P. Stauderman, former editor of *The Lutheran,* will preach at both services on the topic, "Every Day Is News." College students from the area are invited to attend. (30 seconds)

This is conservation week at Good Shepherd Methodist Church, North Main Street, Greensboro. Young people of the congregation have set up collection bins on the east side of North Main Street to receive newspapers, aluminum cans, and glass bottles. Donors are asked to tie up the newspapers in bundles. If you're willing to help in this recycling effort, please bring your papers, cans, and bottles to the collection bins anytime up to Saturday noon. By doing so, you'll help our country and encourage these young people. (30 seconds)

22.
Acres of Diamonds

Statistics indicate that the average American moves every seven years. This form of the "seven-year itch" means that every seven years a new community surrounds your church. While many of the families in your neighborhood will remain in one place for a longer period, you may even now be surrounded by an entirely new mission field. It presents you with a challenge you can't pass up.

This problem is to ferret out the new families and to discover which ones are likely to be attracted to your church. How do you find the new families? One way is to establish a connection with a realtor or real estate office. In every area, lists of real estate transactions are published to indicate what houses have been sold, and usually they give the name of the new owner. Using this material you can easily make your own list of those who have moved within a reasonable distance of your church.

A second method of finding out who's new in the community is through the municipal authorities. Tax lists are available for public scrutiny, either in the local municipal building or in the county offices. You can scan through such lists to find the names of persons in your vicinity who have recently been added.

A third method is to train your members to watch for moving vans! They can tell you promptly when a new family moves into their area. If they are willing to assist further in this matter, they can call on their new neighbors and discreetly find out what, if any, their church preferences are. Such neighborhood calls on newcomers were once a routine part of neighborhood friendliness, but they are now often neglected.

In the case of multifamily dwellings, such as apartment houses or condominiums, the problem is a little more difficult. Security measures usually prevent random calling in such residences. You have to know whom you want to visit before you can even get in. However, here again real estate people can be helpful, since they are often rental agents for the buildings. It may also be useful to establish a contact with the superintendent or manager of the building, who may be willing to give you the names of new tenants.

Once you have a list of names of the people new to your community, one type of approach is to send them information about your church. This should be in the form of a warm letter of welcome to the neighborhood and to the church. Just to send printed materials usually isn't effective, but sometimes an attractive brochure may be enough to inform the newcomer of the presence and program of the church and to open the way for further communication (see sample).

If you have the time and energy, make a personal call at the home of each newcomer to the neighborhood; you'll make many new contacts and will also develop a helpful picture of the social and economic changes that are taking place. You'll find that whether the newcomers are of your faith or not, they will deeply appreciate the interest shown. You can be a sort of personal "welcome wagon" to help orient them to the community. Since you may also represent civic or service clubs, your visits can serve a double purpose.

However you handle it, don't give in to the notion that your community is not expanding and that therefore your congregation does not have an opportunity for growth. Look into the area around your church. You may find a whole congregation of newcomers there. Dr. Russell Conwell raised funds for a great university in Philadelphia by delivering hundreds of times a lecture which he called, "Acres of Diamonds." The lecture was based on the

An attractive folder can introduce your church to your neighbors, to newcomers, and to visitors. This one proved useful to an old, rural congregation in South Carolina.

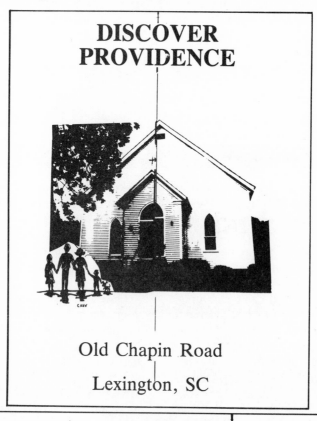

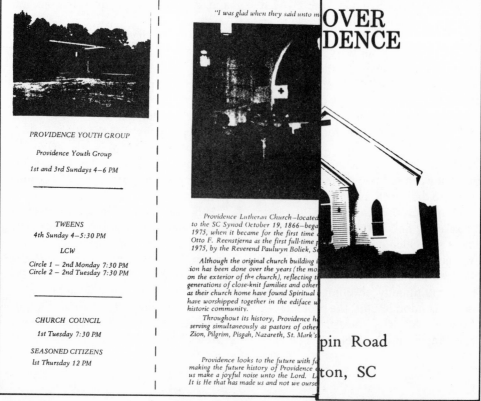

story of a South African farmer who roamed the world in search of fortune, finally returning home to discover that he had acres of diamonds right in his backyard! You may not find acres of them, but you may find one or two.

New people do not move only into new houses or new developments. Even an old, established neighborhood offers a promising field. To reach out into new suburbs and ignore what's happening in the blocks of older houses right around your church is a mistake.

23.
Send in the News

Most newspapers are understaffed. Radio and television stations usually have only two or three reporters who can go out with a microphone or camera to dig up stories. If you wait for these busy people to seek out your church to find out what's going on, you're likely to wait a very long time.

On the other hand, most newspapers are grateful for clean copy which contains useful news or interesting announcements which can be set into type without too much rewriting or editing. Radio and TV stations are also on the lookout for good, lively stories of local interest to beef up their news broadcasts. Some of them even announce special telephone numbers to be used by those who have news to submit.

If you are not getting the amount of coverage you think you deserve, it may be because you are not providing the media with material.

The best public relations director for a church is the pastor, because he or she knows what's going on and usually has some direct contacts with reporters. Often the pastor is too busy to attend to this detail. It's then necessary to find some individual in the congregation who will faithfully undertake to gather, write, and send in news items. We suggest that this be one individual because this makes it simpler to funnel news to the media and also identifies an individual to the media as the contact person when questions arise.

Whether the public relations for your church is handled by the pastor or by some other member, the first step is to recognize what's news. Routine announcements are not news. News concerns itself with the unusual. If the choir is going to sing at the morning service, that's hardly news. But if the mayor of the city is going to be the soloist, that may make up an item. News gets published when it relates to the community, when it interests a lot of readers, and when it contains something of general human interest (see sample checklist).

The next step is to prepare a clear and straightforward news story, including all the necessary facts. There's an old rhyme used to teach journalism students that goes:

> I have six honest serving men;
> They serve me well and true.
> Their names are what and where and when
> And why and how and who.

The very first paragraph of a news story should have six elements: what's happening, where it's happening, when it's happening, and also why, how, and who, to the degree that these are applicable.

A good news story is just the opposite of a piece of fiction. Rather than building up to a climax, it puts all

A checklist of news possibilities

CHECKLIST OF NEWS STORIES

Each of the following has potential news value. When things like this happen in your congregation, get some publicity out of them!

Pastor called
Pastor leaves
Pastor installed
Pastor retires
Guest speaker
Special day program
Vacation Bible school
Church school reopens
Attendance record
Outdoor service
New teachers appointed
New councilmen elected
Election of church officers
Election of club leaders
Members attend district rally
Church redecorated
Week of prayer
Church anniversary
Pastor's anniversary
Thanksgiving service
Reformation Day service
Mother's Day service
Easter dawn service
Christmas midnight service
Letter from missionary
Visit from missionary
Graduates honored
Student recognition Sunday
Visit to every member
Holy Week services
Special musical program
Caroling in streets
Congregational meeting
Year-end report
Sermon on current events

New building planned
Property purchased
Fundraising drive
Groundbreaking for building
Construction progress
Memorial gifts
Completion of building
First service in building
Dedication of building
Mortgage paid off
Purchase of organ
Youth talent festival
Father-Son night or dinner
Mother-Daughter night or dinner
Entertainment projects
Laypersons conduct worship service
Youth conduct worship service
Youth attend summer camps
Youth attend district rally
Report on church school enrollment
Report on membership trends
Children's programs
Fieldtrips for youth
Home-and-school night
Graduation or promotion
New school curriculum
Purchase of special equipment
Adult discussion topics
Special programs at meetings
Visit to county home or prison
Unusual efforts by members
Honors given to members
New organist selected
New church school superintendent
Anniversaries of organist, superintendent

The above checklist includes 70 items that might make news from your church. We didn't include some obvious ones (Pastor elopes with choir director, Church burns down, etc.) because almost everyone will recognize that kind of news!

the important facts at the beginning. Details in the order of their importance can then be added, paragraph by paragraph. Part of the reason for this is that newspapers must fit articles into the space available, and at the last minute because of make-up requirements the last half of a story may be lopped off. If the important news is in the last half, the story becomes worthless. Read an article in a good newspaper, and you'll see that it could be cut from the bottom, paragraph by paragraph, without losing its validity.

Write your story therefore to include all six of the "honest serving men." Tell what was done, who did it, and why, where, when, and how. Your lead might then look something like this:

"The Rev. John Jones of Texarkana will become pastor of First Christian Church in Middletown on September 1. A unanimous vote by the congregation last night issued him the call, which he accepted. He will succeed the late Dr. David Smith, who died last month."

Subsequent paragraphs will tell something about Jones, his age, and background. They may also contain information about the church and its plans when the new pastor arrives. But if nothing more gets into print than the first paragraph, the story remains perfectly valid.

Note also that the item above uses short sentences and clear statements, without needless adjectives. Here are eight points to check in a news story:

1. Get all the facts.
2. Get the facts straight (especially names!).
3. Start from the most important point.
4. Keep it interesting by using quotes, details, etc.
5. Don't leave out anything important.
6. Don't include needless information or editorial comments.
7. Write in short sentences.

8. Use short phrases wherever possible (a "big crowd" is better than a "tremendous outpouring of people").

A news story may be important and well-written and yet not find its way into print. Newspapers have deadlines which they must observe. The Saturday church-news page may be prepared a day early, so if copy for that page arrives at the last minute it may be disregarded. And editors won't put up with eyestrain. A story produced on a beat-up typewriter with a faded ribbon may be just too much trouble to read. Or a story full of scrawled handwritten corrections will take expensive editorial time, more than it's worth.

Therefore, follow good, elementary practices in producing your copy. Find out by a phone call when the story must be in the hands of the editor. Put your name and phone number at the top of the first page. Indicate if there's a special date for which the story is written. Most stories should be for immediate use or for use whenever the paper has space. Leave a few inches of blank paper at the beginning of the story so that a heading or printing instructions can be placed there. Incidentally, don't waste time writing your own headline for the story. This is a prerogative newspapers guard jealously. Double-space or triple-space your story, and leave at least one-inch margins, even if it takes an extra sheet of paper. This permits the editor to make legible corrections where they are needed.

If you'll follow this procedure faithfully, your church will get its share of space in the newspaper. And if the editors know they can depend on you for clean and interesting copy, you may get more than your share.

One further suggestion: if a newspaper or radio or TV station has given you good attention, send a note of thanks.

24.
Tools for the Timid Evangelist

It's nice to have a well-trained and aggressive evangelism committee that can assist the minister by bringing new converts into the fold. But we have to face the fact that in a congregation of five hundred persons, there may be only a dozen who have the guts and gumption to do this work effectively. Most people prefer to remain anonymous and many hesitate to talk about their religion even to friends, much less to strangers. That's why we developed a tool for the timid evangelist.

How can you get all of your congregation involved in the basic Christian duty of evangelism? We developed a three-page folder for them to use called, "An Introduction to our Church" (see sample). The two inside pages describe the work of the congregation and invite readers to attend its services and share in its mission. The third page is a return postcard, with postage prepaid and all ready to mail. It says, "I gave this introduction card to _____." Then there's space to fill in the name of the person who received the folder, along with address, phone number, and church affiliation if one is known. At the bottom, there's a place for the person who gave out the folder to sign.

The folders were distributed to every member with the request that at an opportune time they give the folder to some unchurched friend or neighbor, after having first detached the return postcard. To indicate that they had cooperated, we asked them to fill in the information card and return it to us. That was their total obligation.

The purpose of all this was to encourage the timid evangelist. It's almost the kind of thing kids do on Halloween when they run up and slip something on a doorknob, ring the bell, and run away. The person who gave out this folder could simply say, "I'd like you to think about coming down to my church some time. Here's the information." After that all he or she needed to do was fill out the return card and send it in. The church staff then took over and followed up.

It's a great gimmick for the timid evangelist.

Cut this out, fold it over and you have a topnotch tool for the timid evangelist

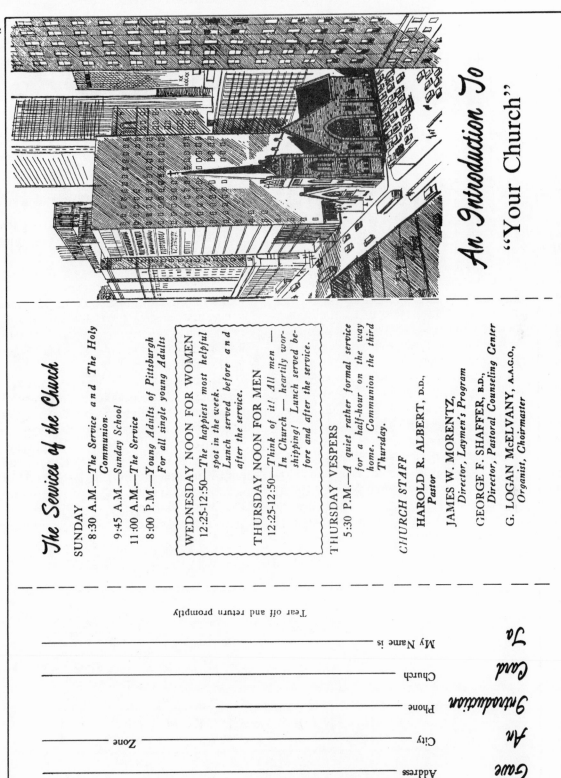

An Introduction To "Your Church"

The Services of the Church

SUNDAY

8:30 A.M.—*The Service and The Holy Communion.*

9:45 A.M.—*Sunday School*

11:00 A.M.—*The Service*

8:00 P.M.—*Young Adults of Pittsburgh* For all single young Adults

WEDNESDAY NOON FOR WOMEN
12:25-12:50—*The happiest most helpful spot in the week. Lunch served before and after the service.*

THURSDAY NOON FOR MEN
12:25-12:50—*Think of it! All men — In Church — heartily worshipping! Lunch served before and after the service.*

THURSDAY VESPERS
5:30 P.M.—*A quiet rather formal service for a half-hour on the way home. Communion the third Thursday.*

CHURCH STAFF

HAROLD R. ALBERT, D.D.,
Pastor

JAMES W. MORENTZ,
Director, Laymen's Program

GEORGE F. SHAFFER, B.D.,
Director, Pastoral Counseling Center

G. LOGAN McELVANY, A.A.G.O.,
Organist, Choirmaster

Tear off and return promptly

My Name is _____

Church _____

Phone _____

City _____ Zone ____

Address _____

Name _____

An Introduction
Gave
Card
To

9

The Challenge of a Downtown Church

WE do not know who you are, what you believe, or to what church you belong. We only know you need the power and Grace of Jesus Christ.

This church offers the warm, friendly ministry of Christ to the business community of Pittsburgh's Golden Triangle.

Snuggled among the skyscrapers we conduct worship services, counsel the distressed persons, administer the Holy Communion, and pause in the midst of hurried errands for moments of prayer.

This is the church with a heart, a smile, and Christ's concern for people.

FRIEND,

- stop in for prayer
- attend a Noonday Service
- kneel for Holy Communion
- call us for help
- join the Sunday morning throng

THIS Church proclaims Jesus Christ as God's Son, Who is the Saviour of us all, the one hope for the guilty confusion and death in which we live, as Luther classically expressed this faith in his explanation of the Second Article of the Apostles' Creed:

"I believe that Jesus Christ, true God, begotten of the Father from eternity, and also true man, born of the Virgin Mary, is my Lord; who has redeemed me, a lost and condemned creature, secured and delivered me from all sins, from death and from the power of the devil, not with silver and gold, but with His holy and precious blood, and with His innocent sufferings and death, in order that I might be His, live under Him in His kingdom, and serve Him in everlasting righteousness, innocence, and blessedness, even as He is risen from the dead, and lives and reigns to all eternity. This is most certainly true."

Through faith in Christ, we live in the forgiveness and p r e s e n c e of God Himself, and through the same Christ, we live with one another.

We cherish the inspired message of the Bible, which brings us Christ, and this Bible is the sole authority of our faith and practice.

We accept baptism, and we frequently partake of the Lord's Supper, because these are Sacraments of God's love and power for our daily lives.

We believe our mission is to share our faith and worship and to proclaim Christ in our downtown location every day in the week to the throngs of business people and the passers-by.

First Class
Permit No. 9659
Pittsburgh, Pa.

BUSINESS REPLY MAIL
No postage stamp necessary if mailed in the United States

Postage will be Paid By—

First Lutheran Church

615 Grant Street

Pittsburgh, Pa.

25.
Picture Your Church

Your church needs a recognition factor. In your community, when people hear the name of your church, they should immediately be able to identify it and know where it's located. The way to develop this kind of recognition is by constant repetition of things like the church's name, address, and motto ("The Friendly Church"), or something similar. While you may be bothered by the insistent repetition of television commercials, they represent an investment of millions of dollars by major corporations in order to develop just this kind of instant identification.

A recognition factor can be developed for your church in dozens of ways, and no single way will be 100 percent effective. Only by using every available means of impressing on your community the fact that your church exists to serve its people will you build up its status as a community institution which everybody knows.

One simple method you can start with is to place a directional sign at the nearest busy highway. People who drive by will be alerted to the existence of your church even if they have no direct interest in it. Many will say, "I never knew that there was such a church in this community."

Denominational supply houses have attractive special signs which are used nationwide to identify their particular church body—Episcopal, Lutheran, United Church of Christ, Church of God, etc. If you can't use this identification, get a signmaker to produce a simple metal sign with an arrow pointing in your direction and lettering of the name of your church and the distance to it. It might say something like, "Faith Chapel. Two blocks south." The distance is important so that people know they don't have to go miles out of their way to reach your church, and also so that they don't drive past it.

Be sure to get permission to set up the sign, especially if it is placed on private property. Your aim is to make friends, not to lose them.

Another factor in developing recognition for your church that costs a little money but is well worth it is the publication of colored picture postcards (see samples). These should bear a picture either of the church building, the interior of the church, or whatever other pictorial feature is most attractive. In every area of the country, there are printers who specialize in producing this type of material. Such cards must usually be ordered in large quantities if you want a good price, but don't worry about this. They're good for several years and have many uses.

Obviously the picture you choose for the card is of utmost importance. It should have good color and must put your best foot forward. You may have a camera enthusiast in your congregation who can make a sharp color transparency. If not, hire a professional photographer.

The postcards can be displayed in the entrance hall or foyer of your church, where members and visitors can pick them up. Sometimes a small charge is made for them. The cards are also good advertising when mailed out from the church or its organizations to members in honor of their birthdays, anniversaries, or other personal events. Members of the congregation will treasure them as mementos of their church and will also want some to mail to friends.

The promotional value of the postcards needs to extend beyond the wall of the church, however. Have someone take a batch of the cards to all stores in your vicinity that normally sell picture postcards. Place a few of the cards depicting your church among the other cards. Storekeepers may be willing to pay for the cost of the cards placed on their racks, since they'll charge customers for them, but even if they don't it's a good investment. Your church's picture is right up there along with the other postcards showing the prominent buildings and natural splendors of your area.

Your church's picture has other uses. Some churches publish and sell Christmas cards which bear a picture of the church altar wreathed in its Christmas decorations or a picture of the church building in a winter setting. Others have correspondence stationery with the church's picture on it.

Billboard advertising can also sometimes be used to your advantage. The outdoor advertising company that has the franchise for such displays in your area may occasionally have unsold billboard space. They'll work with you to put up a poster advertising your church and permit it to remain until they again have a commercial buyer for the space. Some denominational agencies may be able to provide you with a ready-made poster to put up on the billboard. If you make your own billboard sign, be sure it is in good taste and attractive. If the sign is done poorly or amateurishly, it can be self-defeating.

Advertising in newspapers and other media is also important in establishing recognition for your church, but this has been dealt with adequately in earlier chapters.

Postcards spread recognition for these churches, whether they're big buildings in a city or modest ones in the suburbs.

Section III
Increasing Knowledge

26.
Fill Those Empty Chairs!

Empty pews in church and empty chairs in church school are a liability. They're discouraging because they indicate that a place has been prepared for someone who did not think it worthwhile to come. To fill those empty places is a constant challenge.

But what about church school, particularly in the lower grades? You can't conscientiously persuade members to produce children more rapidly in order to fill the empty chairs. As a matter of fact, our declining birthrate has made these empty spaces a problem in public education as well as in our churches. Yet, during the church school hours in any community you can find many children wandering about or playing in the streets when they ought to be receiving religious instruction. How can you reach them and bring them in?

We decided that children themselves are the best persuaders of other children. That led to the creation of the Order of St. Andrew.

It began in the primary department (first three grades) with the recounting of the story of Andrew, the disciple of Jesus who brought his brother Simon Peter into discipleship. Every child, boy or girl, can be an "Andrew" by bringing someone to hear about Jesus, and the first step is to bring them along to church school. We therefore urged the children to invite others to come with them to learn about Jesus, but to make sure that they weren't taking children away from some other church or persuading them to do something of which their parents might disapprove. We promised that every child who brought another would become a member of the Order of St. Andrew and be allowed to wear a special ribbon during the church school session signifying this distinction.

It worked! It became a matter of pride for the youngsters to tell others about their church school and to *bring* them along. In some cases, parents followed!

At each session, the children who had brought others were singled out for special attention, and the special ribbon was pinned to their clothing. The ribbon sash simply bore the word "Andrew" on it. The sashes were easily made from three-inch-wide packaging ribbon, preferably white. The ribbon was cut into eighteen-inch lengths. We applied gold or

63

silver gummed letters to the ribbon or simply wrote the word "Andrew" on it with a crayon or Magic Marker. These ribbons became cherished possessions to the children and were doubtless reward enough, but they also enjoyed the added value of having some of their weekday playmates along with them in Sunday church school.

At one session when the "Andrews" were called forward, one youngster started to cry. He hadn't brought anyone along and felt badly. His teacher comforted him and was surprised to hear him say, "I asked a lot of kids, but I couldn't find one called Simon Peter." Naturally that problem was quickly ironed out. For the benefit of this youngster and all others, a clear explanation was given that anybody could be "Andrew" and anybody could be "Simon Peter."

Before the end of the year, the Order of St. Andrew had forty members and more than that number of newcomers had been enrolled. Not only had the children themselves helped fill up the empty chairs, but they had at an early age been given an excellent experience in witnessing and evangelism.

27.

Warm Up Your Bullpen

One of the secrets of success for a professional baseball team is a good bullpen. The bullpen is the place on a baseball field where relief pitchers warm up. The term also may refer to the relief pitchers themselves. With a good bullpen, a capable substitute can be rushed into the game whenever the starting pitcher tires or loses control.

Yale's famed homiletics professor, Dr. Halford Luccock, once jokingly suggested that setting up a similar bullpen in the rear of the church might spur preachers on to greater achievements. If the person in the pulpit began to tire and get wild, Luccock said, he'd see the substitutes warming up and ready to replace him. That would give the preacher the incentive to do better—or else.

The application is not only to preachers. There are times when faithful church workers get tired or feel they are in a rut. If there's a good substitute available, it may save the day.

Our congregation required a large teaching staff for the Sunday school. It wasn't easy to persuade nearly a hundred excellent teachers to give their time and efforts week after week, year after year. And most were too conscientious to take time off, leaving their pupils in the hands of someone who was not well prepared. Some prospective teachers also told us they'd take responsibility for a class only if they could take time off now and then. In addition, some very capable teachers could no longer promise to be present every Sunday, but offered to keep abreast of the lesson plans and to substitute when needed, particularly when we could give them some advance notice.

We therefore organized the latter group into our bullpen. They kept warmed up attending teachers' meetings and were always provided with the current material. There were only six or eight of them, but that was enough. They made it possible for us to respond affirmatively when prospective teachers said, "I'd be glad to assist, but I can't promise you every Sunday." The substitute list was made available to those teachers. Then, if a teacher was not able to come because of a business trip or a family event or other proper reason, he or she could call a qualified substitute. It made for a smooth-running Sunday school. The bullpen worked.

Another problem was finding male teachers, especially for the older boys. Many youngsters had had only female teachers in the lower grades and somehow had gotten the impression that teaching in Sunday school was a job limited to women.

Since ours was a suburban congregation, the majority of the children were brought to Sunday school by their parents in the family car or sometimes in carpools. One Sunday I wandered around the parking lot and saw that in a half-dozen cases the father of the family had driven the youngsters to Sunday school and was either snoozing or reading the Sunday paper during the class hour. (We were unable at that time to have adult classes during the Sunday school period, because with an enrollment of six hundred children we filled every bit of space in our cramped quarters!) I took time on several Sundays to sit in the car alongside the father-driver for a few minutes to talk with him about the needs of our Sunday school and the opportunity for male teachers to inspire the lives of adolescent boys. My success was not great, but it worked in at least three cases, and they turned out to be three of the best teachers we ever had. In some other cases, the drivers offered to join the bullpen.

Our Sunday schools rely on the faithful and devoted service of teachers who are present week after week. When they find themselves in circumstances which may prevent them from coming every week and therefore reluctantly want to resign from the teaching staff, offer them an alternative. If you have a good bullpen, you can still win the game.

28.
Invitation to Learn

Structured educational opportunities like Sunday school, weekday school, adult Bible classes, and vacation schools meet most of the educational needs of our congregations, or so we think. However, the learning process goes on everywhere and at all times. Many school children learn more during recess periods or in locker rooms than they do in their classes. College students will tell you that extracurricular activities are often more productive and practical than their regular courses.

We need therefore to seize every chance to turn a casual meeting into a learning experience for those present. There's ample biblical precedent for this, especially in the life of Jesus.

In a church in West Palm Beach, Florida, a large group of senior citizens met regularly under the sponsorship of a Golden Age Club for a weekly luncheon. The luncheon, partly funded by a government agency, was nonsectarian and open to any older citizens who could attend. Because some of these people had plenty of time on their hands, they would drift into the church hall an hour or more before the luncheon, spending the time just sitting, chatting, and sometimes getting in the way of the cooks.

The church's pastor occasionally dropped in to greet the group. One day one of them suggested, "We waste an hour or more here every week. Why can't we spend it in Bible study or in some discussion?" As a result, the pastor agreed to lead off an hour's discussion prior to each luncheon, assisted by some capable leaders from the group itself. Since this could not be a typical denominational Bible class, it developed into a discussion group on major issues of the day, with the background question being, What does the Bible say about this? Topics could be taxation, health care, provision for the elderly, crime, international affairs, and the like. In the course of a year, the discussion hour became an important element in the lives of many of the elderly people. The church's teaching ministry had a new dimension.

Because of the time available to them, senior citizens are a ready-made audience for Bible study or topical discussions. But there are other neglected opportunities. Trying to reach more business men and women of the community, one suburban church decided to hold prayer breakfasts during Lent. Business men and women were invited to come for an early breakfast, during which there was Bible study, discussion, and prayer. The sessions broke up in ample time for those attending to get to stores or to the trains that took them downtown to work.

For a downtown church, something similar may be worked out at lunchtime (see sample). In the business district of a city, it's hard to find a place for a comfortable, reasonable, and quick lunch during the noon hour. In Pittsburgh, as mentioned elsewhere in this book, a congregation profited by establishing a weekly luncheon at which business people could eat and also participate in a brief service of worship. In New York, a midtown church invites business people in for a light lunch, during which there's dramatic or musical entertainment with a religious message.

In some communities, women of the church meet on weekday mornings for sewing, quilting, or just conversation. Such groups have found their sessions enhanced if some learning program is provided. Even if one of those present simply reads from Scripture or from some religious publication while the others are busy sewing or whatever it is that they do, the time is better spent and the church's teaching is expanded.

Railroad commuting to work is still in fashion in some New York suburbs. Thousands travel daily by train from suburban Long Island, Westchester, and New Jersey to their places of employment in Manhattan. On Long Island, local ministers arranged to hold weekly Bible study sessions in one of the railroad cars during Lent. They found that many commuters crowded into that car to take part and make their otherwise boring journey something more helpful. A similar program was arranged for New Jersey commuters. In both cases the railroad officials were cooperative, but they did expect the ministers to purchase tickets like all the other riders!

Educational opportunities abound. Be alert to those around you. What would otherwise be wasted time for many people can often be converted into an invitation to learning.

29.
Diplomas for Everybody

Featured among the wall decor in many homes are marriage certificates, diplomas, or other mementos of great events in life. Among treasured possessions packed carefully away for future generations, one may often find baptismal certificates, attendance awards, and similar memorabilia. People place high value on such evidence of their participation. Also, such items often have value in establishing legal claims and birthdates, among other things.

Don't neglect the "token" that accompanies a big

Noonday Services

LENT

"Your Church"
3119 W. 6th Street
Los Angeles, California

Wednesday Noons

FOR MEN AND WOMEN

12:25-12:50

Lunch served before and after the Service.

THEME:
"Discipleship in Business"

✝

February 15
"Like a Rock"

✝

February 22
"The Price Tag on Love"

✝

March 1
"The Glad-Hander"

✝

March 8
"I Doubt It"

✝

March 15
"I Hate Him"

✝

March 22
"The Traitor"

Dear Friends:

Lent is the time to re-affirm your disciple-ship. Amidst the busy pace that we set in our day to day living all our good intentions often fall by the wayside. Now during this Lenten season your Lord says to you, stop, "I am the way, the truth and the life."

This church invites you to accept the many opportunities for enrichment of your spirit-ual life during this Lenten season. So that this church may serve all people, the sched-ule of services is arranged throughout the week at various times for your convenience. Through this wide ministry we serve busi-ness people (noon-day services), our congre-gation (all services), those who seek under-standing (Wednesday Bible study), those who seek to know the faith of this church (Pastor's Class). Spiritual growth comes through understanding and witnessing. Dis-cipleship means understanding God's will and being a witness to your fellowmen.

Come, worship, grow that this Lent may be a time for the deepening of the Spirit and concern for your Lord and your fellowmen. "By this all men will know that you are my disciples, if you have love for one another." (John 13:35)

Your Pastor

✝

The Church is open each day for private prayer.

The Lenten Pastor's Class

A series on the Christian faith with full opportunity for questions and discussion—giving you opportunity to learn something of this church and the responsibilities of membership. Six sessions beginning Sunday, February 12. New members will be received March 26.

Noonday Lenten services held by a downtown church for business people open new avenues of service and bring new people into the church. This folder opens out, serving as a poster to place in restrooms and on bulletin boards in business establishments.

NOONDAY SERVICES

Every Wednesday 12:25 – 12:50 Sharp
Mid-Week Services for Business People

BEGINNING FEBRUARY 15

(ASH WEDNESDAY)

"Your Church"

6th Street at Shatto Place   **(1 Block East of Vermont)**
PASTOR

LUNCH SERVED BEFORE AND AFTER THE SERVICES

. . . For all people who look to God! . . .

event in the life of an individual. Long after the event itself is forgotten, the certificates or diploma will still be on display.

Most congregations routinely provide certificates for a baptism, confirmation, or wedding. They are important documents. But it's equally important to give recognition to other milestones, which often helps heighten their standing in the view of the participants.

For instance, give a "diploma" to the children who pass from one department of the church school into another. When the children leave kindergarten to move into first grade, this may be one of the biggest steps they've taken in their lives up to that time. It should be recognized! Some enterprising congregations even make a ceremony out of it, dressing up the tots in caps and gowns for their "graduation day" from kindergarten. Parents with cameras delight in recording this event for the family album.

In our congregation, children were introduced to the Bible as soon as they could read. However, moving from the primary department's third grade into the intermediate department was a major event, since it meant going from one building which housed the "little kids" into another building where the older students met. We therefore held a sort of graduation ceremony on the promotion day when this move took place. As a token of the event, we presented each child with a Bible, suitably inscribed, which was to be his own. Such Bibles were purchased very reasonably from the American Bible Society. They became lifelong treasures for some of the youngsters.

Don't stop with the children. Adults like recognition, too. Teachers who have served faithfully and effectively during the year deserve some accolade. At the close of the year or at some special service, present them with a certificate of appreciation for their work. In our case we had nearly 100 teachers and staff workers in the Sunday school, so each fall we designated a Sunday at which they attended the church service to be given special recognition. This included presentation of the certificates. While it was only a token, it helped make them feel that their efforts were appreciated. Their attendance as a group also opened the eyes of some other church members to the work that was being done.

Choir members also need encouragement. They ought to be given their special day. Sometimes a small lapel pin is presented to choristers who have assisted in the services for a year or more. But it's easily possible to take a sheet of music manuscript paper and have someone with expert penmanship or who is skilled in calligraphy make it into a certificate of appreciation worthy of framing.

Showing this kind of special appreciation for your teachers, ushers, choir members, and other church leaders helps to encourage their continued efforts. It also gives a special flavor to some Sunday when the service might otherwise be routine. It's worth doing.

30.
Put Your Bulletin to Work

In most churches, an usher stands at the door, gravely handing out a bulletin to people as they enter. The bulletin contains, among other things, the order of the service. It lists the hymn numbers, the Scripture readings, and the sermon topic, plus some assorted announcements. It may sometimes look very ordinary and unexciting, but it's potentially one of the most important tools available to instruct people and to spread information about your church. It is actually a weekly newspaper devoted to the affairs of the congregation.

Yet, after a service is over, many of the bulletins are simply left in the pews. Others remain stacked up on a table at the entrance, because they've never even been given out. When this happens, an important tool is being neglected.

The first thing that needs mention is the importance of the appearance and format of the bulletin. Often, prepared bulletins are purchased from a church supply house or provided by a denomination. Some of them have very attractive covers. Generally they come as flat 8½ by 11 sheets which can be folded into a leaflet, and three of the four resulting pages are blank, awaiting your imprint. What's put on those pages makes a lot of difference.

If you buy prepared bulletins, shop around for something distinctive. Most of them are standard. They have a pretty picture on the cover and that's nice, but it doesn't do a thing for your church! Have your third-grade class draw a composite picture of your church (or of the pastor!) and put that on the bulletin cover, and you'll stimulate a lot of excitement. Or if you have artists or photographers who can provide something unique, by all means use them. Just a little imagination can make your bulletins something special that will be talked about—and looked at.

Unless you have a very large congregation or a very inexpensive local printer, the material you provide for the bulletin is probably printed by mimeograph. These handy machines have been greatly improved in recent years and can produce a printing job that's almost equal to photo-offset or letterpress printing. But you'd never know this from many bulletins. Imprints are uneven, smudged, and sometimes illegible. This need not be tolerated. Electric typewriters are inexpensive and cut evenly into the stencil. Mimeograph makers provide instructions for the operation of their products. Even illustrations can be easily included.

This isn't the place to provide detailed technical information on cutting stencils and operating mimeographs. But it is the place to ask you to take a critical look at the product your church office is turning out and to make sure that it looks as good as your church deserves.

Format and content of the bulletin are also a subject that has been covered well in dozens of pamphlets and books. A few suggestions may be in order, however Make sure your bulletin contains useful information, clearly presented. A bulletin is not intended to be another chapter in the Holy Scriptures, but sometimes it contains enough pious repetitions to make you wonder! And readers should not have to unscramble confused sentences in order to find out what you're telling them. Present your information simply, clearly, and directly. Read the stencil or the first copy with care so that you can make corrections and avoid bloopers. If words are misspelled, names omitted, or grammatical errors permitted, it denigrates your church at least among better educated readers.

But let's assume that your bulletin is attractive, well written, and informative; yet people simply glance at it to follow the service and then throw it aside. What can you do to rescue it?

1) Ask worshipers to take the bulletin home with them and give it to a neighbor or friend who might be interested in seeing something about what goes on at your church. This is a casual but effective form of evangelism.
2) List in the bulletin daily Bible readings or daily prayer themes and ask worshipers to take the bulletins home so they will have a daily reference and reminder.
3) Distribute the bulletins to Sunday school children or members of adult classes who may not be present at the worship service. Children whose parents are not regular churchgoers will in that way be messengers who bring into the home the news of the church.
4) Collect all leftover bulletins at the close of the service and use them as calling cards wherever you visit, even at the service stations or stores. Hand a bulletin to a storekeeper and say, "I just thought you might like to know what's going on at our church." Chances are the response will be far beyond your expectations. One storekeeper in such a situation phoned the next day to ask, "How can I put an ad in your bulletin?" We told him that he couldn't, but that he could pay for the bulletins one Sunday and we'd mention his contribution in the bulletin. His check came promptly!
5) Mail extra bulletins to absentees from church, to neighbors of the church, and to potential members. Neighbors of the church are often happy to know in advance about your programs, even if they do not participate. Sooner or later they may!
6) Send your weekly bulletin to the local newspaper or to your regional reporter for the newspaper. And send it to any local radio station. Some enterprising reporter may pick up news items which will then appear in print or be announced over the air.
7) Send the weekly bulletin to the regional reporter for your denominational magazine or to other religious publications in which you have an interest.
8) If you have space available, print a couple of quiz questions on the Bible or on religious issues, with a note that the correct answers will be printed the following week. Advise people to keep the bulletin so they can check their own answers against the correct ones. Once this idea catches on, you've got a steady readership, and the assurance that there'll be lively household discussion about your bulletin!

31.
Your Newsletter

The written word has been an important adjunct for the church ever since ancient scribes began recording the sayings of the prophets. The advent of the printing press was a boon to religion, and the first printed matter consisted chiefly of Bibles, religious tracts, and theological works. Even today, amid the torrent of material that floods from printing presses, religious material is a major component.

Churches use the written or printed word so much that the technical quality of what they produce deserves more attention than it gets. Both the appearance and the content of printed matter tells a lot about your church and about you. Whether it's a pastoral letter, a weekly bulletin, an annual report, a newsletter, or a magazine, it needs to be well-written, attractive in appearance, easy to read, and directed toward the personal interests of the people who are expected to read it.

Only a generation ago, a typewriter and a mimeograph were the chief tools for congregational publications. With easy access today to photocomposition and photocopying, every congregation has a wide variety of possibilities. Photos and drawings can be easily reproduced; so can news clippings or facsimiles of any kind. The only limits are those of your own imagination!

The chief form of communication for most congregations, aside from the preaching and teaching of the Word, is a periodical newsletter or magazine. To do its job well, such a publication must be lively and entertaining and a good publishing job, as well as a conveyor of information. It needs to demonstrate the dignity and importance of the congregation's mission, but at the same time it should never be stuffy or overly pious. And remember, it has to compete with daily newspapers and a host of other publications for the reading time of your people.

In view of the caliber of some parish publications, you wonder why they are continued. One which I see regularly consists chiefly of homilies and scoldings from the pastor. It is not an inviting example of Christian love. Yet for this congregation, it evidently has enough value to justify the time and effort put into it, as well as the cost.

The top achievement for a church newsletter is to heighten a feeling of belonging by acquainting members with one another and giving them a sense of being part of a "family." Another aim for the newsletter is to develop interest in the church's program and a desire to support it in cooperation with other members. A third purpose is to alert members and friends of the congregation to current activities and to encourage them to participate in them. There must also be some space given to routine matters, such as reports of meetings and of treasurers, but to allow such things to fill most of the paper is to doom it to the pile of unread "literature" that swamps the average household.

Develop a style for the newsletter that's conversational, talking to people as you would talk to them on a friendly visit to their home. That's the key to making the newsletter a success. People will then reach for it as eagerly as they would reach for a letter from a friend.

Personal notes, news and information about other members, and chatty comments about topics of current interest in the congregation help make the newsletter readable. For instance, a brief vignette of some member can be included in each issue. You'll find many members with interesting occupations or backgrounds. To tell about them and their work helps introduce them to others and opens the way for greater fellowship within the congregation. Such items need not be limited to the rich or famous— somebody's service in caring for neighborhood children or in developing a new recipe for potato salad for a fellowship dinner can make a good story. Even brief "social notes from all over" can help keep members in touch with one another and can stimulate the desired "family feeling" in your congregation.

A personal experience may prove how this thing works. During World War II, I determined to keep in personal touch with the young men from my parish who entered the service of their country. At first this was possible, but by the second year they were scattered around the globe. To write them personally would have taken all my time. We assigned families of the parish to write to each of the service men (later, women), but this didn't work well, either.

I therefore started a mimeographed paper, sent out monthly (at least) to all the service personnel on our mailing list. It was called *The Banner,* with the title coming from a Sunday school hymn most of them knew: "Fling out the banner, let it float, skyward and seaward, high and wide." But even though it was mimeographed, I made sure that *The Banner* was like a personal letter, filled with news about the community, about their neighbors, and about the church. Later, as responses came from the service people themselves, we could publish a full page of excerpts from their letters in each issue, thereby keeping them in touch with one another.

The little paper attracted great attention. It was passed around in military camps. Chaplains wrote asking for copies, and boys not from our congregation asked to be included in the mailing list. It gained such attention that about one year after its inception the prestigious *New York Times* published an article about it under a two-column headline that read: "Teaneck Pastor Publishes Newspaper for Fighting Forces of Congregation." The article read, in part:

In the early stages of the war the Rev. Albert P. Stauderman decided that he would maintain a steady correspondence with the young men who left his congregation for the armed forces and for a while he had no difficulty. But as the number of departed boys grew he realized that unless he devised a simplified plan he would have to give up his correspondence, which he was loathe to do, because the boys and their parents had expressed appreciation for what he was doing for their morale.

Having been a newspaper man before entering the ministry, he got an idea. He would write a news sheet which, while it was less personal to the individual men, would nevertheless carry all the hometown and church circle gossip along with his own special message. . . . "It is distinguished chiefly for its chatty style and has set the pattern for numerous imitators, many of which are far better," he said. "My little mimeographed sheet of three pages goes all over the world, to marines in New Guinea, a lieutenant colonel in the Solomons, a Navy lieutenant on a minesweeper in the South Pacific, to boys in Oran, Casablanca, Alaska, London and to several points in the United States. We now have 82 men in service from our congregation. The circulation of our next issue, however, will be 84 because since the last issue two young women have joined the service."

The pastor says he knows the boys appreciate the news sheet because he receives a constant flow of letters. In addition, he's gotten letters from ministers in many parts of the country asking for copies of the sheet in response to requests from their boys who saw *The Banner* in their respective camps.

The lead article in each issue is the pastor's greeting, a condensed sermon. Then follows the "local gossip" as he calls it: ration problems, erection of the town's honor roll, church news, and finally notes culled from the letters of the boys themselves so their friends all over the world will be able to keep up with them.

By the time we retired our service flag, two years after the end of the war, it had one hundred ninety-seven stars on it, including two gold stars. *The Banner* had done its work well in keeping us in touch with our service men and women. It was easily converted into a parish magazine, published to this day.

The secret of its success can make any church newsletter a success: talk to people in simple terms about themselves, their friends, and the things that they are interested in.

32.

Learn from Your Neighbor

"An idea belongs to the person who uses it best," said Dr. Paul Scherer. Remember this when you seem to run out of ideas or when you need mental stimulation. There are lots of good ideas floating around, and the secret is to latch onto them and adapt them for your own use.

Examining the publications of other congregations can often help you improve your own. You may find that they are doing things in a more effective way—perhaps in makeup, organization of material, or in the mechanical process of printing. Don't be too proud to learn! You can be sure that *Time* keeps an eye on what *Newsweek* is doing and vice versa.

One plan that has been widely used is for each minister to bring copies of the bulletin or newsletter from his congregation to a meeting of the local ministers' association. These copies are then passed around and shared. Sometimes there's a general critique of the publications. Just a chance comment from someone can be a means of making radical improvements in a publication. And sometimes an entire session may be used to analyze and suggest restyling or contents changes for one publication.

If there's no such local organization, collect bulletins and newsletters from other churches whenever you can. Perhaps your members can solicit copies from relatives and friends who attend other churches. One pastor asks vacationers to send him a copy of the bulletin from each church they attend during their summer trips. He says he gets many good ideas from these papers. On occasion he has displayed all the bulletins at a meeting of the church council or the church cabinet, asking those present what format they like best and what features ought to be adopted for their own church bulletin.

Learning is not confined to church publications. Churches in a given area face similar problems and deal with similar types of people. If there are churches in your area that have been singularly successful in handling some local situation, inquire into their program and see if it can be adapted to your own congregation. Imitation may be flattery, but often it is also good common sense. If all churches are working for the ideal of faithful witness and service to their Lord, they ought to be helpful to each other rather than feeling that they are in competition.

Sometimes this spirit can lead to tremendous ecumenical growth. For example, in one community three recently organized congregations—Lutheran, Methodist, and Seventh-Day Adventist—were all in the process of planning church buildings. Costs were high and prospects for an adequate edifice were discouraging until someone hit on a wonderful idea. Why not pool their resources and build one structure that would serve all three? Each congregation could have its own offices and meeting rooms, while sharing the church sanctuary and the fellowship hall. There were questions and difficulties, but in a spirit of Christian sharing, the plan was worked out successfully. A much finer and more useful building was constructed than would have been possible for the individual congregations, and the cost was less than half of the total of what would otherwise have been spent. The biggest problem was the arrangement of worship hours when the church sanctuary would be used, especially on festival days, but the Seventh-Day Adventists had their own schedule and the Lutheran-Methodist combination was worked out to everyone's satisfaction.

Not everything will be resolved so dramatically. But in your case, here are a few suggestions:

1) Obtain and study the Sunday service bulletins of neighboring churches to see if you can improve your bulletin by adopting some of their features.
2) Obtain and study newsletters from other congregations. They may have program suggestions that you could use in your congregation.
3) Examine the worship schedule of the best attended congregations in your area. If their people come out more strongly at a different hour from that of your services, maybe you should consider a change. For example, a Lutheran church in Bronxville, New York, made a survey of its families and found that 60 percent of its members planned to be away weekends in June, July, and August. It therefore transferred "Sunday" school to Wednesday evenings during those months, with good results. If your parishioners also scatter on weekends, you may want to try something similar!
4) Check into the community service program of other churches. If they attract a lot of your young people by sponsoring a Little League team, for instance, maybe this is the sort of thing your congregation should be doing.
5) Read up on the plans and programs of outstanding churches in your denominational magazine or in current books. Some of the things they are doing may be useful in your program, even if you operate on a simpler scale.

33.

How to Wake Up Your Sunday School

Most major denominations have in recent years reported a sharp decline in enrollment in religious education programs, especially Sunday schools. Many churches no longer have a thriving adult Bible or discussion class, or a complete educational program for adult members. While there are still some good-sized Sunday schools, they don't begin to reach all the potential Sunday school pupils in the community. Millions of children are not receiving religious education in any form.

Are you satisfied with the number of adults in learning situations in your church? And is your educational program for children reaching its goals?

At First Lutheran, a downtown city church in Los Angeles, we had all the problems. The Sunday school program was faltering, and teachers were becoming discouraged. Our members attended worship services faithfully, but seemed to overlook the educational opportunities. And when the adults failed to attend, the children often had no means of getting to the church.

To draw attention to the fact that Sunday school is important, the congregational leaders decided to try to engender some excitement about the educational program and to try to stir up the notion that something big was happening or about to happen. So they closed the Sunday school for July and August!

Of course, a lot of Sunday schools are closed during July and August anyway, so that hardly was a noteworthy event. But in their case the school had normally been open every Sunday of the year. This time they turned July and August into a four-week leadership training course, mandatory for all teachers, but with identical programs for each month, so that teachers could choose which one to attend and thus avoid conflict with their own vacation programs.

During this time they laid out the curriculum for the entire year. Each teacher was thus able to see the teaching plan and contents for all the grade levels. All departments used a regular thirteen-week cycle, including the adult segments. For the adult classes three courses were to be offered during each thirteen-week period, enabling adults to choose the topics likely to be of most interest to them. The approach to the adult group was, "There's got to be something here that you are interested in." With three thirteen-week cycles, each containing three courses, there were nine courses offered for adults during the year. They felt at least one of these courses would have enough appeal to each adult to get him or her out for at least one thirteen-week period. If adults were unwilling to commit themselves for the entire year, they could at least come for one of the cycles. Many adults did commit themselves to just one of the thirteen-week cycles, but once they got into the courses it wasn't too difficult to keep them coming back.

The entire teaching program was then laid out in a little catalog, rather similar to college or school catalogs (see sample). It listed the courses for all age groups, with a short description of each course. This made a rather elaborate sixteen-page booklet, but the same result can probably be achieved on a more modest scale by a mimeographed outline of the courses.

The booklet was called "Invitation to Learn." In addition to the outlines of the courses, it carried a message from the pastor urging all members to regard the educational opportunities as much a part of their church commitment as the worship services. The concluding paragraphs said,

You will note that the courses have been stressed and not the teachers. A list of teachers will be made available before each series of courses is offered. All teachers have been trained in an intensive preparatory course. Excellent leadership is therefore offered.

Now it is up to you. Like the farmer who must thin out the seed so that a mature crop may be realized, so the church member must cut out lesser interests and put worship and study together as the first requirement on Sunday morning. Give yourself and the members of your family the opportunity to learn by accepting this invitation to learn! On Sunday, let us go to the house of the Lord and learn together how rightly to handle the word of truth.

The program was all-inclusive. It included pastor's classes for future members, the teen-age groups, and went all the way down to the tiniest tots in the nursery. It was intended to show that education is a continuing process and one that deserves high priority in the parish. For this reason, a great deal of time was put into preparing the program and the brochure. It also revealed to the congregation that teachers were willing to attend training sessions and to prepare for their classes. Through regular promotion it tried to prepare people for the novel process of making a personal commitment to an educational program in which they would know in advance the theme of the classes and the dates for the courses.

It was a great success. When the Sunday school closed for the summer previous to this program, it had seven persons attending the adult class regularly, one of those typical classes with seven little old ladies. When sessions resumed in the fall, one hundred fifty-five persons were enrolled in the adult education section in the three different classes. During the year it slowed down a little, but even for the third thirteen-week series the adult group had dropped only from 155 to 130, which is not bad! If you want your Sunday school to wake up, you must invest some time, money, and imagination, and you've got to deliver a good program.

An attractive brochure (cover only is shown here) outlined the courses offered in the revised educational program at First Lutheran. The 16-page pamphlet may be more elaborate than you need, but a simpler version will help tell people about the content and aims of your educational ministry.

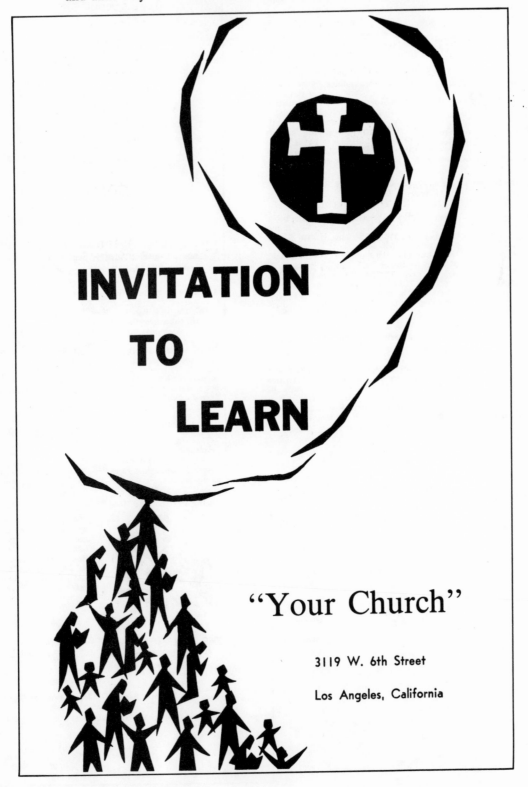

INVITATION
TO
LEARN

"Your Church"

3119 W. 6th Street

Los Angeles, California

THE PRIMARY DEPARTMENT — ages six, seven, and eight (Public school grades 1-3).

"The Bible and Christmas" . . . Sunday, September 24 through Sunday, December 31, 1961

Three basic and important units comprise this quarter. "Using the Bible" is the first unit. Children receive training in handling and reading the Bible. The next unit, very appropriately, contains "Some Stories Jesus Told." Careful use of children's language awakens their imagination to vital parables of Jesus. A Thanksgiving session is included. A beautiful Christmas atmosphere features "Christmas in Many Lands," the third unit. Recognition of the world-wide church is established by attractive, appealing sessions.

"Jesus the Savior" . . . Sunday, January 7 through Sunday, March 25, 1962

We need to make clear to little children that Jesus the baby, Jesus the boy, Jesus the man, and the Savior Jesus are one and the same person. This is the objective of the first unit, entitled "Jesus Grew Up." The unit is designed to help overcome this often found confusion, which sometimes persists into adulthood. The next unit, "Christian Children in Their Neighborhood," provides training in the social relationships of children. The final three sessions begin a unit, "God and His Son Jesus," which carries over into the spring quarter. Coming at Eastertime, it is intended to guide primary children into simple understanding of the ministry, crucifixion, and resurrection of Jesus.

"God's Great World" . . . Sunday, April 1 through Sunday, June 24, 1962

First three sessions of this quarter complete the unit, "God and His Son Jesus," which was begun in the last quarter. Activities of the apostles after the Day of Pentecost feature the second unit, "Helping Jesus in His Work," in which there is a missionary theme. Thanksgiving and praise to God for his blessings which make the world wonderful, useful, and beautiful establish the theme for "The World God Has Given Us," title of the final unit.

6

THE ADULT DEPARTMENT — three courses offered simultaneously, beginning Sunday, September 24 through Sunday, December 31, 1961. (Select one only.)

Augsburg Uniform Series — "Christian Growth"

This course is based on New Testament teachings about Christian growth. Such growth includes experiences of increasing knowledge, control, sympathy, love and service. It is stimulated and nourished by Bible study, meditation, prayer, worship, group fellowship, self-discipline, and devotion to the Christian enterprises. Attention is given to hindrances to Christian growth such as doubt, egotism, self-righteousness, intemperance, and personality problems. Consideration is given to both personal and social maturity. Christian maturity is not a status to be attained but is a process and growth into Christ-likeness.

"The Book Of Life"

This masterful survey of the whole Bible gets at the heart of the Scriptures without the clutter of unnecessary detail. The material is clearly organized, and the chapters so carefully written that they deserve reading and rereading. The text gives a view of the Bible as a whole.

"Being Christian At Home"

A course related to Christian family living. Such matters discussed are: Christian conversation at the table, prayer in the home, the family Bible, the religious development of children, children and discipline, fun and laughter in the home, family finance, and family relationships to the community.

THE ADULT DEPARTMENT — three courses offered simultaneously, beginning Sunday, January 7 through Sunday, March 25, 1962 (Select one only.)

Augsburg Uniform Series — "Jesus And The Ten Commandments"

This course shows the relationship between the Old Testament

11

Section IV
Increasing Income

34.

Hallowed Ground

Buying property? You may have a splendid vision of a beautiful church being erected on what's now a weed-covered vacant lot, but others may have trouble visualizing the opportunity. They are more likely to see it as an expense that can be postponed until some future time. Convincing them of the need to raise funds for the purchase of empty ground for future expansion is always difficult.

At St. Paul Church in Teaneck, we had an added problem. We were in the midst of a mortgage-reduction campaign when vacant property adjacent to ours came on the market. A friend in town hall tipped us off that an absentee owner was willing to sell the 150 by 150 plot at a reasonable price. We needed the space for future expansion if we hoped to stay in the area, but we didn't have the money, and the mortgage on our building was already a burden.

We knew that sometimes a church building fund has been bolstered by selling "bricks." Purchasers of each brick contribute a specific amount to the cost of construction, and usually a wall chart depicts the bricks and identifies the purchaser. We thought of doing something similar, by making a plot plan of the property and "selling" each square yard. With twenty-five hundred square yards to sell, we could ask a couple of dollars each and perhaps get at least enough for the down payment! But we realized also that some people might want to claim "their" square yard of the property, which might be divisive.

We therefore decided not to sell specific sections, but to sell the soil itself. In that way, each donor would feel that his or her contribution made possible the entire purchase. It would also invite larger gifts, which was important since the buy-a-brick idea, involving thousands of individual purchases, would pose bookkeeping problems.

To implement this decision, we mapped out a campaign that would enlist the whole congregation in the purchase of the property and also follow good stewardship procedures. We prepared a four-page folder, the cover bearing the legend, "Hallowed Ground." The second page was a letter from the pastor, explaining the plans for future expansion and reminding members of the need for space both for building and parking. The letter told of the opportunity that had come up and warned that if the adjacent property was sold for housing and built upon, the chance for our church to expand in its present location would be lost.

The real gimmick came on the third page. We obtained hundreds of cellophane envelopes, about two inches by four inches—the kind pharmacists sometimes use for pills. Our young people spaded up some dirt from the new property and sifted it, then spooned an ounce or so into each envelope. The envelope was stapled to the third page of the folder, with a brief statement below to the effect that this soil would be hallowed forever as a site for a house of worship. It asked each member to purchase his or her share of the "hallowed ground."

While the little envelope with the soil was intended only as an attention-getter, we found that it had added meaning in some cases. Some people brought back the soil and rather reverently placed it on the newly purchased ground. Others kept it as a reminder of their part in the purchase of the lots!

To make this kind of promotion effective, the envelope containing the soil must be transparent. If a cellophane envelope is not currently available, a little package can be made by using a piece of plastic wrap about six inches square. Place the soil in the center, then fold over the plastic in such a way as to fashion an envelope, fastening it with a staple as you attach it to the folder. In this way, the soil is immediately visible to the person who opens the folder.

Variations of "hallowed ground" may also be helpful. In Philadelphia, a civic group devoted to the preservation of old historic buildings needed funds to purchase and maintain them. During the course of some restoration work at Independence Hall, the group was able to obtain one of the original old beams. This was cut into pieces about one inch by three inches and about one inch thick. These pieces were then distributed to members of the group with the appeal that a contribution be made in return for possession of an original piece of Independence Hall! The appeal was successful.

Keep it in mind when you're faced with the need to raise some extraordinary funds for the purchase of land, or for construction or restoration of buildings. When you need an alternative to a burdensome mortgage debt, sell your soil, not your soul.

There are unlimited variations to this kind of fundraising procedure. A newspaper note says, "Ohio State University football fans have been invited to buy souvenir chunks of the artificial turf from the Buckeyes' stadium in Columbus, Ohio. Pieces of the 8-year-old turf can be bought for $5 a square foot and $25 a square yard to help defray the cost of replacing the carpet." Well, if they can do it at Ohio State, think of the possibilities when your church carpet needs replacing!

35.
Little Things Add Up

One of our major food chains at one time advertised, "A penny a pound profit." Current prices, especially of meat, make it seem more like a dollar a pound profit. But the secret that successful merchandisers have discovered is that a consistent, small profit is better than an occasional windfall. One of America's largest fortunes was built on nickel-and-dime sales by stores that once claimed they sold "nothing over ten cents." Other products have become successful by insuring repeat buying or because they trained customers to get into the habit of shopping for certain items in certain places.

Translating this into the life of the congregation, we need to develop in people the habit of giving. Consistent giving is the basis for good support for the mission of the church. Who is the better giver, the member who comes to church once a year and flamboyantly places a $100 bill on the plate, or the family that sets aside $1 each day for the work of the Lord? You know the answer.

Good giving habits are usually ingrained early in life, most often by parental example. Training children to give is important. However, children as well as adults need to know the reason why they are giving and what they are giving for. This means bringing stewardship training right down into the early grades of Sunday school.

It also means that children learn to make contributions out of their own money. Money for their gifts ought to be earned at home or by doing chores for others. It should be money actually earned and therefore a personal gift rather than one which was just handed over to the child by parents. Making gifts with money they actually worked for helps children to grow in their concept of stewardship. The money can come from their own allowance or as the product of some service they have rendered to others.

In order for children to make their gifts personal by having worked for the money, the projects they support must be scaled down. Children are loving and sympathetic, and they enjoy the satisfaction of meeting some need which they can understand. For instance, a relief agency may report that a starving child in a refugee camp can be fed for fifty cents a day. Children will find joy in raising this amount. It's a figure within their comprehension, and by helping another child they're doing something that seems to apply to their everyday life. A Sunday school class might "adopt" such a refugee child for one day each week and set this as a goal to which the children would contribute.

Pennies and nickels and dimes therefore still have a place in the scheme of Christian giving! To stimulate children for this, a Los Angeles school set up a scale to weigh children, asking them to make a pledge on the basis of a penny a pound. Every month children would get weighed and be given a "pledge card" with their weight, which would be their "pledge" for the month. For example, one child might weigh forty-eight pounds. His "pledge" for the month would then be forty-eight cents. The great part of this program is that it teaches children stewardship in its purest and simplest form. As you grow bigger, you grow up. As you grow up, your responsibility as a steward grows. As you grow, so does your responsibility to others. This is a long, slow, but subtle lesson learned over a period of years that the child will never forget.

A simpler variation of this can be the birthday bank, which also holds attraction for youngsters. Birthdays are big affairs when you're eight years old. It's fun to be called forward in Sunday school and have the whole group share in a prayer for your birthday. As those celebrating their birthdays are called forward, all those present join in a birthday prayer or song. After all, a birthday marks another year of God's grace.

To share their birthday with others, children are asked to give one penny for each year of their age. The pennies go into the bank, which at the close of the year provides a fund to be donated to some special cause, particularly one that benefits children. In a large Sunday school, the birthday fund can amount to quite a bit.

Teachers and leaders should be included, too, but their contribution doesn't have to give away their exact age! In one Sunday school, the pastor always responded to the birthday appeal by putting a dollar in the bank, which started a rumor among the kids that he was a hundred years old.

If possible, some small birthday remembrance should be given to each child. It may be just a woven bookmark or some other inexpensive but meaningful item. These things are treasured.

Carrying the idea a little farther, many congregations profit from pennies (or dimes or quarters) by distributing Advent or Lenten banks, or similar collection devices for daily use in the home. One large national mission agency offers plastic banks in the form of a loaf of bread. When these banks are filled and brought to the church (usually as a contribution toward easing world hunger), they are broken open. The bread and the breaking of bread has an added spiritual significance. But there are also cards to hold coins of various sizes. These devices can provide an added source of income for a congregation and its causes, while at the same time they develop among the people the concept of regular, daily giving. It's excellent stewardship training, providing a reminder right within the home of the blessings God gives us each day and of our duty to return thanks, praise, and offerings daily as well.

36.
Alternatives for Every-Member Visitation

Although most denominational stewardship programs call for an annual visit to every household to solicit gifts and pledges for the congregation, this can become a tiresome and needless effort. It's a waste of good people's time, and it's really not necessary. Visiting all members every three years, with thorough preparation and an attractive presentation, is much better. Then the visitors aren't tired, and the people who are visited don't become bored by hearing the same old story year after year.

But if there's no visit to each member, there must be some attractive alternative to produce the needed pledges and to stimulate increased giving by the congregation. By using two such alternate programs, a three-year stewardship cycle can be worked out for everyone's benefit.

The first alternative to personal visits is obviously a campaign by mail. The chief element in such a campaign is to attract attention and vigorously persuade people to make a response. A striking pledge card sent out with a letter signed by the chairman of the stewardship committee can work effectively. The letter should be brief and to the point. (The card and letter are sampled at the back of the book.) The letter should come from the church council or the stewardship committee and should be on behalf of those groups, not from the pastor. After all, stewardship solicitations are not the pastor's prime responsibility. It's far more effective when laypersons can witness to their own stewardship, stating their own commitments and calling for a similar response from others.

In such mailings, save money by using the least expensive nonprofit postage rate available from the postal service, currently about three cents. But to distinguish any mailing from your church from ordinary junk mail be sure to have some attention-getting message on the *outside* of the envelope. You don't want your important letter thrown away unopened! A sticker saying "Important news from your church" or something similar will work wonders. Or you can use a colored envelope. Maybe you can borrow a leaf from magazine solicitors and tell people in advance to be watching for a message from their church.

The card sampled here was professionally prepared, to lead the reader from the first words right through to the last, with a big question mark on the cover and the question: "Tell me why?" The overleaf bore the answer: "God gave himself." Then comes the personal appeal: "How much of myself will I give? Of my Sundays? . . . My weekdays? . . . My money?" The purpose of this approach was to reverse the usual order and refute the reply of some individuals that "All you want is my money."

The card asks a threefold pledge. What are you willing to do in the line of worship and Communion? What are you willing to do in the line of personal commitment of time and talent for work in the church and the community? And then finally, how much money are you willing to devote to the cause?

The card was very well received during the years when we used it in our congregation. Only a few members failed to respond, and they were then visited in person. But most members felt that it was good stewardship of time and energy to "visit" in this fashion rather than through a massive and time-consuming every-member canvass.

A second alternative we used to the annual membership canvass was "10%." Starting early in September, every item that went out from the church or was distributed at services carried the teaser

PLEDGE...?

TELL ME WHY!

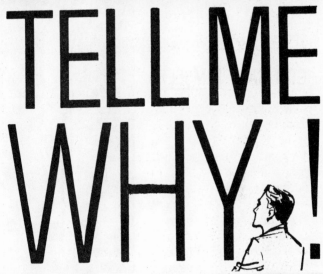

YOUR PLEDGE IS ALTAR-BOUND
Fill it out and bring it with you on
LOYALTY SUNDAY, NOVEMBER 19.

Your presence will be a witness to your faith.
Your pledge will be a measure of your faith.

"Your Church"

THIS RAISES MORE QUESTIONS,
DOESN'T IT!

10% 10% 10% 10%

Cut this out carefully,
fold it twice
and you'll have a novel
and effective pledge card

GOD GAVE <u>HIMSELF</u>...

HOW MUCH OF <u>MYSELF</u> WILL I GIVE?

OF MY SUNDAYS?

☐ In church for worship.
☐ In church for Holy Communion.

OF MY WEEKDAYS?

☐ I'd like to do something.
☐ Interested in_____

OF MY MONEY?

$_____weekly_____

or $_____(other)_____

▼

Write name_____

Address_____
　　　　　　　　(Street)

_____
　　　(Zone)　　(City)

Telephone_____

Pledges may be increased or decreased
at any time by writing the church office.

please see reverse side . . .

Brief, personal, and to-the-point, a stewardship letter like this can do wonders in evoking an affirmative response.

"Your Church"

Dear Friend:

I didn't pledge last year. I'm going to pledge this year.

I discovered being responsive to God's love is not enough. You have to be responsible to His church. If pledging makes the church more effective, who am I to withhold a pledge?

I love my Lord. I love His church. He pledged forgiveness of sin and eternal life.

God gave *Himself*. — That is why I am going to pledge this year.

How much of *myself* will I give?

That's the real question.

Sincerely,

On behalf of the
Church Council

Dan Thellman
Stewardship Chairman

P.S: I'll see you in church on Loyalty Sunday, November 19, with your pledge.

"10%" stamped or written on it. It was always the same, for easy identification—just the numerals and the percent sign. One way to handle this is to buy a few rubber stamps of varying sizes, from a tiny quarter-inch to big three-inch characters. Using these, stamp everything that goes out with the insignia "10%." EVERYTHING. Even envelopes carrying mail from the church office or routine announcements of meetings should be marked.

At first, no one was told what it meant. Gradually, people began to get the idea that we were talking about tithing, and when people think you're talking about tithing, they tend to get a little bit frightened, which is just what we wanted. All through September, every item carried the mark 10%. All through October, the campaign continued. Finally, in the usual stewardship-emphasis period in November, we let the cat out of the bag. The revelation was then made that we were NOT talking about a tithe, wholesome as that form of giving may be. What we were asking was for all givers to increase their gifts by 10 percent.

Our experience has been that many people go beyond this. If they have been giving one dollar a week, they won't raise to $1.10. If they have been giving two dollars, they won't go to $2.20. It's too difficult to pledge odd amounts. So if they've been giving one dollar, they'll say, "Make it $1.25." Or if they've been giving two dollars, they're likely to raise it to $2.50 or $3. Our experience was that the figure was almost always rounded off to the high side, not to the low side! And people who are already giving generously find it easy to accept a 10 percent increase. People in the higher brackets of giving always seem to find it easier to increase their commitments!

These two alternatives permit a three-year cycle for the every-member visit. They remove the unfairness of calling the same people, year after year, and sending them out to tell the same story over and over again. Having the visit at three-year intervals permits a freshness of approach and a change of pace that everybody welcomes.

37.
Using Human Resources

Nothing really happens at a person's sixty-fifth birthday except that the "birthday child" can qualify for full Social Security benefits and is all too often out of a job. A strange myth in our society insists that someone who is sixty-four years and three hundred and sixty-four *days* old is employable, but one day later becomes expendable.

Each year a greater proportion of our population joins the ranks of those over sixty-five. Senior citizens constitute an enormous, but often unused, human resource for society and for churches. Churches

especially can benefit from this resource because these people are usually economically secure, thanks to pensions and government benefits. They are therefore able to offer their services at low cost or at no cost. When senior citizens are employed for church work, the benefit is two-sided. It helps the congregation or church agency because extremely capable, dependable, experienced, and innovative individuals are available at little cost. But it also benefits the individuals, because one of the chief needs in retirement is for retirees to find some wholesome, productive kind of activity which they can responsibly undertake. For their own mental health, they must feel that they are useful to society.

The real challenge in your parish is to match the jobs to be done with the persons best qualified to do them. In some cases, retired persons are willing to take on big responsibilities, but others prefer to minimize their responsibility in order not to be tied down too much. And, of course, both the needs and abilities of retired persons change over the years.

In one parish, the minister decided that he did not want an ordained assistant, but would prefer a lay assistant who could handle many of the administrative details, especially the routine and time-consuming ones. In the search for such a person, the ideal answer was found right in the congregation. A retired business executive, a widower in his early 70s and in excellent health, needed an occupation with responsibility. He was already fairly well versed in parish affairs, and he looked forward eagerly to resuming a nine to five office routine, provided that he could have freedom to come and go as he wished and could have ample vacation time.

The parish had five fulltime employees—the minister, two secretaries, a nursery school teacher, and a sexton. The coming of the business manager aided all five of them, relieving them of the need to attend to details like purchasing materials, paying bills, keeping records, and coordinating their work. To make the arrangement thoroughly businesslike, the business manager was "salaried" at a fraction of what he would have earned in a similar capacity in the commercial world. And everybody was happy.

But there's only one such place in a parish, and there are very many retired people. How can they all be used?

In your area there are doubtless social mission or health agencies that can use more volunteer workers. Such agencies may serve some of your members. Some agencies have directors of volunteer services, who recruit and train volunteer workers who are willing to give at last a few hours each week. Volunteer work of this sort is rarely a fulltime job, but is limited to a few hours for a day or two each week, out of consideration for the age and energy of the workers.

Volunteers serve by calling on shut-ins, delivering hot meals if there's a "Meals on Wheels" program, serving as drivers to ferry handicapped persons to hospitals or clinics, doing simple office work, and preparing and serving food. To participate in such service requires that the volunteers have not only the desire to help, but also sufficient dedication to be present and on time when needed.

Your congregation can fit into such volunteer programs and also strengthen its own work by appointing some efficient person as a director, or coordinator, of volunteer services. The job of such a person would be to make contact with agencies in the area that use volunteer helpers, find out what talents are needed and what the requirements are for service. The next step is then to establish contact with all available retirees in the parish, telling them of the needs. If they offer to volunteer for service, a list of names and the special abilities of each person can be drawn up and maintained.

This list will be an asset to your own program. For instance, among those willing to work may be some who are good cooks and who list food preparation as their avenue for service. If they will agree to take responsibility for purchasing, preparing, and serving food, why not encourage them to set up a monthly hot luncheon or dinner program open to all retirees and senior citizens, and provided at cost? The luncheon or dinner program will perform a valuable health preservation function for the older folks, many of whom are either unable or unwilling to prepare a proper dinner for themselves, particularly if they are living alone. But it will also bring people into your church who might not otherwise be drawn into your program.

On the list of volunteers you may also find former teachers or librarians, who will make themselves available to read to shut-ins or to write letters for people who are physically unable to do their own writing. Or the former teachers may be willing to tutor some child who needs and deserves such assistance.

Your most efficient church secretary may come from this pool of retired persons. Crackerjack secretaries are hard to find, and not every congregation can afford to hire one. Yet there's always work in the church office for those who can type letters, operate office machines, post accounts, or even just fold letters and stuff envelopes. You won't have just one secretary, of course. A group of volunteers, perhaps with each one working in the office one day a week, will be your secretarial "team." To avoid confusion and to designate responsibility, you may find it best to assign a particular task to each individual—one to prepare and print the church bulletin, one to post financial records, another to keep the address list. In this way, each will have a particular responsibility, and you'll eliminate the old excuse, "Oh, I thought Jane was going to do that!"

Another way in which retirees can be employed to assist the pastor directly is as friendly visitors. They won't go out to sell anything or to solicit anything, but just to be cheerful links between the congregation and its members. Some can be assigned to visit those who are housebound, who can't go out much because of physical limitations and who are therefore often bored and frustrated. Ministers visit such people regularly, of course, but the visits can become repetitive and difficult for the pastor. To hear the same story over again every week is a high price to pay for a pastoral visit! A volunteer visitor may be the answer. A person with a pleasant personality and an interest in people, especially one who is a good listener, can visit at least occasionally in the pastor's place. The variety in such visits will be pleasing and helpful to everyone involved.

Retirees with special skills may also help solve some special problems for the parish and its members. A retired lawyer, for example, may be helpful in counseling with persons about their wills or their legal affairs. A retired carpenter or plumber can be worth his weight in gold to a congregation if he will periodically inspect and repair the property.

Time and planning must go into setting up an efficient parish program that involves retired persons in volunteer service. But by establishing such a program, you are enlisting many years of experience and know-how worth a great deal and costing you very little. At the same time, you are contributing to the mental and physical health of retirees by insuring that they are needed and useful. It's too good a program to pass up!

38.
Visit Every Member, Every Two Weeks

Keeping in touch with your members is important, but it's not easy or cheap. With postal costs constantly increasing, to send out a message every two weeks would cost almost a dollar a year in postage alone even at the most favorable third-class rate. Add the prices of envelope, paper, and secretarial work, and it becomes a big item. It's also time-consuming and would require very innovative contents to get people to read it.

Yet there's an easy way in which congregations can reach their members every two weeks, or at least every month, at low cost. Better yet, they are reached with an attractive, colorful, and lively publication which supports the mission of the church and encourages their participation in it. The way is by using your denominational magazine.

Most denominational magazines have special reduced rates for congregations that subscribe for all member families. For example, the most widely circulated such publication, *The Lutheran* of the Lutheran Church in America, costs only a little more than two dollars a year to go into the homes of members twice each month. Other denominational magazines offer similar plans. If no reduced-rate plan is indicated in a publication you'd like to share with your members, write to the magazine and suggest one.

If your denomination has no suitable magazine,

there's a wide diversity of other publications that can represent you. The Associated Church Press, Evangelical Press Association, and Catholic Press Association include more than a thousand member publications, so there's almost sure to be one that fits your congregation's needs. Every church leader subscribes to some of these periodicals. Look them over and choose one that you think best for your situation.

To make such a magazine a real pastor's helper in your parish, it must be delivered directly to the homes of members. A bulk subscription sent to the church and handed out to those who attend serves little purpose. You want especially to reach those who do not attend regularly or who are "fringe members" of the parish. These are the ones who chiefly need the stimulus provided by the regular arrival in their homes of the magazine, which is a reminder to them of the congregation and its work.

In typically active parishes, pastors cannot visit every member twice a month. In most cases, they can't bring a message of cheer or comfort to sick or aged parishioners so frequently. Even if they could visit every home every other week, they would not be able to keep all the people continually informed on the far-flung activities of the church at home and abroad. They could not keep up with the many issues affecting religious life which arise in church-state or economic circles. They would be embarrassed to emphasize on every visit the financial needs of the parish and of the larger church. But all these things can be done effectively and graphically by a denominational magazine or by one of the major inter-faith journals.

39.

Fair Enough

Our congregation, like many others, had a traditional fall bazaar. Women of the congregation started early in the year with their knitting, crocheting, and sewing—aprons, doilies, scarfs, placemats. Others began collecting various kinds of loot from merchants. Some stuff was purchased from wholesale outlets. Then as the time for the bazaar neared, posters were distributed throughout the city and preparations made for the special dinner, offered at a bargain price. Since other congregations were having the same kind of bazaar at the same time, there was competition.

In the bazaar week, the men of the congregation came on Monday to set up booths. Tuesday was decorating day. Wednesday the merchandise was placed on the tables and the kitchen crew was working to prepare food. The bazaar started Thursday evening and continued on Friday. The biggest money-maker was always the dinner, since the price undercut any restaurant in town, and also because the women were good cooks. When the last shreds of merchandise were cleared away late on Friday, we had made a few thousand dollars, everybody was worn out, and it appeared that the same people who had made the special gifts had also bought them.

"We need the bazaar to pay our winter fuel bills," the church council members said. "The congregation wouldn't be able to get along without it."

But we began to wonder about the whole process. Was this good Christian stewardship or a cop-out? Didn't it persuade people *not* to give, when by buying a $10 dinner for $3.50 they thought they were making a contribution to the church? But others cited the fellowship value of the bazaar. They said it brought members out for a social evening and enabled them to work side by side in a mutual effort.

Then one year the minister, with the approval of some influential members, made a proposal. "Let's cut out the tiring and questionable bazaar and simply ask people to make a direct contribution of the same amount they would normally spend there," he suggested.

"It won't work," was the general answer.

But we tried it.

Early in October we sent out a letter to all members. It was headed in big letters, "Fair enough!" The letter went on to say that income from the annual fair was important to the congregation, but that the practice of selling goods to support the church was poor stewardship and the work the bazaar entailed for a small group of people was an unfair burden. It said that a small direct gift from every member would provide more money for the church than had ever been raised by the fair. There would be a congregational social gathering in early November, the letter continued, at which such a gift would be requested. This procedure would be "fair enough" for everybody.

A few weeks later we sent out the offering envelope and the invitation to attend the social gathering. We decided to call the event the "Harvest Festival," and we held it on the anniversary date of the congregation's organization, November 8. For entertainment, we got a prominent speaker and hired a professional magician. We also engaged an accordionist who was an accomplished song leader. Our men's group offered to serve coffee and cake at the close of the program. Then we waited to see what would happen.

A half hour before the scheduled start of the program, the hall was already filled. Some latecomers had to stand outside. Hasty trips were made to bakeries to find more cake!

Many contribution envelopes were returned that night; others were put in the plate on Sunday. When it was all tallied, we had several hundred dollars more than had been made by the previous year's bazaar. Beside that, everyone was happy to be relieved of the chores associated with the bazaar, and most felt the evening of fun, fellowship, and song was far better than that of the bazaar.

The second time around is always a more severe test! But on the second year of our Harvest Festival, a nonmember, whose family attended our church, offered to match the amount we received in contributions. He had been successful in business and felt that this was a way of showing his gratitude. So we wound up with twice as much money as a bazaar had ever produced. After that, the Harvest Festival was a permanent fixture for the congregation, and people began to look forward with anticipation to the evening's program.

Because of the potential income from the event, we felt we could afford to spend generously for the entertainment program. This insured competent professional performances. In addition, some congregational groups staged comic skits, and these were often far better (and more hilarious) than the professional presentations.

If your bazaars are dragging everyone down and if you are fed up with such commercialization, test the will of your people to give directly. They can still have as much fun as a bazaar provides—and more. They'll agree that this alternative is "fair enough."

40.

Where Does the Money Go?

Not all appeals made in the name of religion are honest. Some television "evangelists" have gotten a bad reputation because of their constant requests for money, which then is used only to further their own broadcasts. As people become aware of such shady practices, they become suspicious of all requests for contributions. Legitimate appeals for funds suffer because of the shysters.

Some national committees attempt to monitor the performance of individuals and organizations that make direct charitable appeals to the general public. They urge that those seeking donations for charity should report publicly the proportion of their income that goes for salaries, advertising, promotion, and other overhead. Some states have laws that compel fundraising groups to report their earnings. The laws usually allow a very generous amount—up to 35 percent—to be used for promotion, advertising, and administration.

Every congregation should learn from this the need to provide a clear, honest financial report to its members. By doing so, giving is encouraged.

A simple and easy-to-understand way to do this is by a pie chart. Such a chart consists of a circle, representing the total budget. In proper proportion, this pie is then divided into pieces, with each piece showing the percentage of the total used for a specific purpose.

Segments of your congregational pie should show what is used for the preaching and teaching ministry, maintenance and upkeep of the church property, utilities, local missions, worldwide or denominational missions, mortgage reduction, fellowship programs, and whatever other major items go into your budget.

When there are special appeals outside of the budget, make them specific. To give "for the work of the Lord" is commendable, but people will dig down a little deeper when they can visualize just what their money accomplishes. Don't merely ask for more money, but ask that specific and definite needs be met.

One congregation needed more space for its worship programs, and the council decided to embark on a fundraising program for a new building. "When we see how much people will give, we'll know what kind of a building we can erect," they said. The campaign flopped badly. A few years later they called in a professional fundraising counsel and explained their predicament. "The first thing you need is a picture of your new building and a set of plans," the counselors said. "You can adapt the plans later, but people give better when they can see what they're giving for."

In one rather affluent congregation, the pastor took time one Sunday morning to tell of a poor family he was trying to help. One child in the family desperately needed dental work that would cost hundreds of dollars. He described the situation well, but did not actually ask for a penny. Yet before the congregation had filed out of the sanctuary that Sunday morning, he had received more than enough money for the dental work, plus many offers of additional assistance for the family. When the people of the congregation could visualize a need, they responded promptly and adequately.

Givers also often feel more rewarded when their contributions are applied to specific purposes. If they're trying to raise funds for an organ, let individuals donate a special set of pipes or a particular keyboard. It gives them a feeling of participation which increases their willingness to respond. A good example of this kind of directed giving is found in the great success of several organizations which support homeless children overseas. Donors to these groups are assigned a specific child and can even correspond with the child they "support." This is specific, personalized giving and it pays.

There's an old saying that if you need something, tell God and tell God's people. You can add to that, tell them also what their gift will purchase or accomplish. When people know what they are giving for, they will respond to the utmost of their ability.

Don't Put This Book Down

Don't let all the ideas in this book lie on a shelf; put them into action. We think you will need to order more books for all the other leaders in your church who could profit from these ideas. Buy additional copies of this action book from your local bookstore.

Now tear out the samples you need and get something started! The first page you tear out may be crucial to your future. If you ever watch Johnny Carson, you know "Everything you ever wanted to know about how to get a church into action" is *not* in this book. So . . . send us your ideas.

One final word, short cuts lead to short circuits. If you try an idea, go all out, do it all. If you do half a job, you will achieve half a success, and that's the same as half a failure.

The church has had enough of that. Do it right and succeed in a big way. Success is not unchristian. God loves a winner too.

Good luck and God bless you. If you try everything in this book, you'll need both good luck and God's blessing; but at least try.

Al and Jim

Put this letter (or the one on the next page) on your church stationery, sign it personally, and see if it doesn't draw a far better response than a cold and formal announcement! It can be adapted for any important meeting in your congregation.

Dear Friends:

You and I probably agree completely on the importance of religion in our lives. Without the guiding love of God, life wouldn't be worth much.

And we agree, I'm sure, on the value of the work being done by our church. Its influence in the community and in our lives is a constant source of inspiration.

Only the church can't go forward all by itself. To be sure, our gifts help it. The pastor does a self-sacrificing job serving its people. But it takes more than that. It requires our personal interest and our individual contributions of time and energy to keep our church progressing.

One small thing you can do to help the church is to attend the annual congregational business meeting on Monday, January 23, 1981, at 6:30 P.M. At the meeting we'll discuss our program, hear about plans for the year, and make our commitments for the work that is to be done. A dinner will be served before the meeting. Your reservation can be sent in on the enclosed card.

I hope you'll agree with me that your most important engagement on January 23 is at the congregational meeting. See you there!

                                                        Signature

Dear Friends:

A wise man once said, "Eternal vigilance is the price of liberty." Within our lifetime we've seen examples all over the world of situations where people just didn't care enough and as a result lost liberty, and sometimes even life.

To keep your political liberty, your responsibility as a citizen is to vote at election time and to keep informed about your government. That's part of living in a free land as a free citizen.

Religious liberty isn't being threatened by any foreign power. Religion in our land is respected by almost everyone. But when people become indifferent and neglect their responsibility for their churches, religious freedom can be misused or at least weakened.

Your responsibility as a church member is to take an active interest in what's going on in your church. Only in that way can you protect your wonderful heritage of Christian freedom.

Don't take a chance on losing one of your most precious possessions. Attend the annual meeting of your congregation on Monday, Jan. 23, 1982 at 6:30 P.M. in the parish hall. Dinner will be served and reservations can be made on the enclosed card.

We'll be expecting you on January 23.

Signature